Double Sided Pages

Merry Christmas

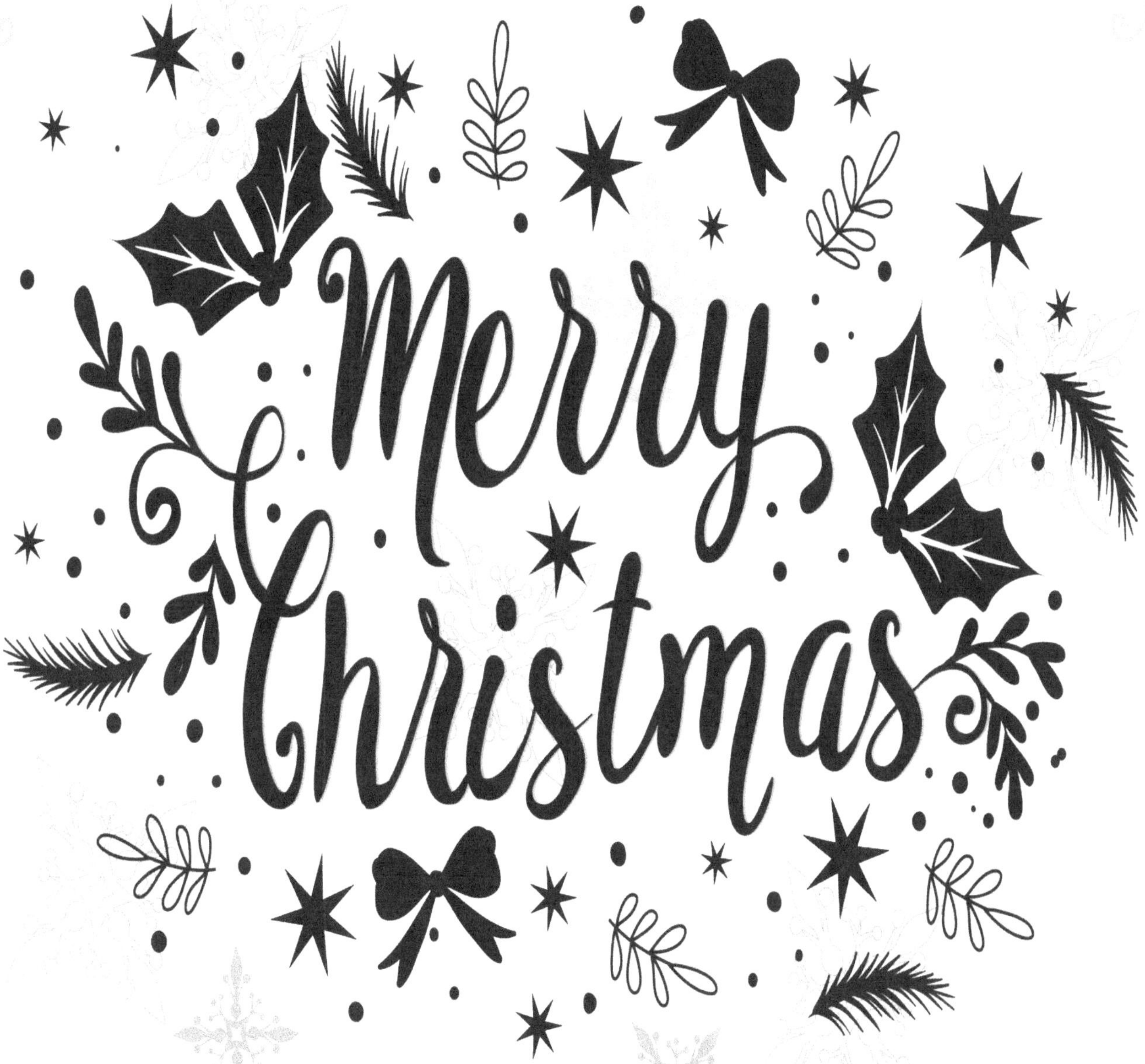

Adult Coloring Book

MERRY CHRISTMAS
By
Ravenswood Publishing
Copyright © Ravenswood Publishing 2017
Cover Copyright © Ravenswood Publishing 2017
Published by Gaia's Essence
(An Imprint of Ravenswood Publishing)

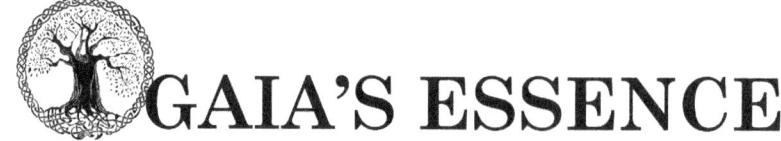 **GAIA'S ESSENCE**

This book is a work of non-fiction created entirely for entertainment purposes. All pictures were created with combinations of free clip art from various sources. All images are creations of the author and are copyrighted.

Ravenswood Publishing
1275 Baptist Chapel Rd.
Autryville, NC 28318
http://www.ravenswoodpublishing.com
Email: RavenswoodPublishing@gmail.com

Paperback orders can be made through Createspace
http://www.createspace.com

Printed in the United States of American
First Edition
10 9 8 7 6 5 4 3 2 1

ISBN-13: 978-1981231195
ISBN-10: 1981231196

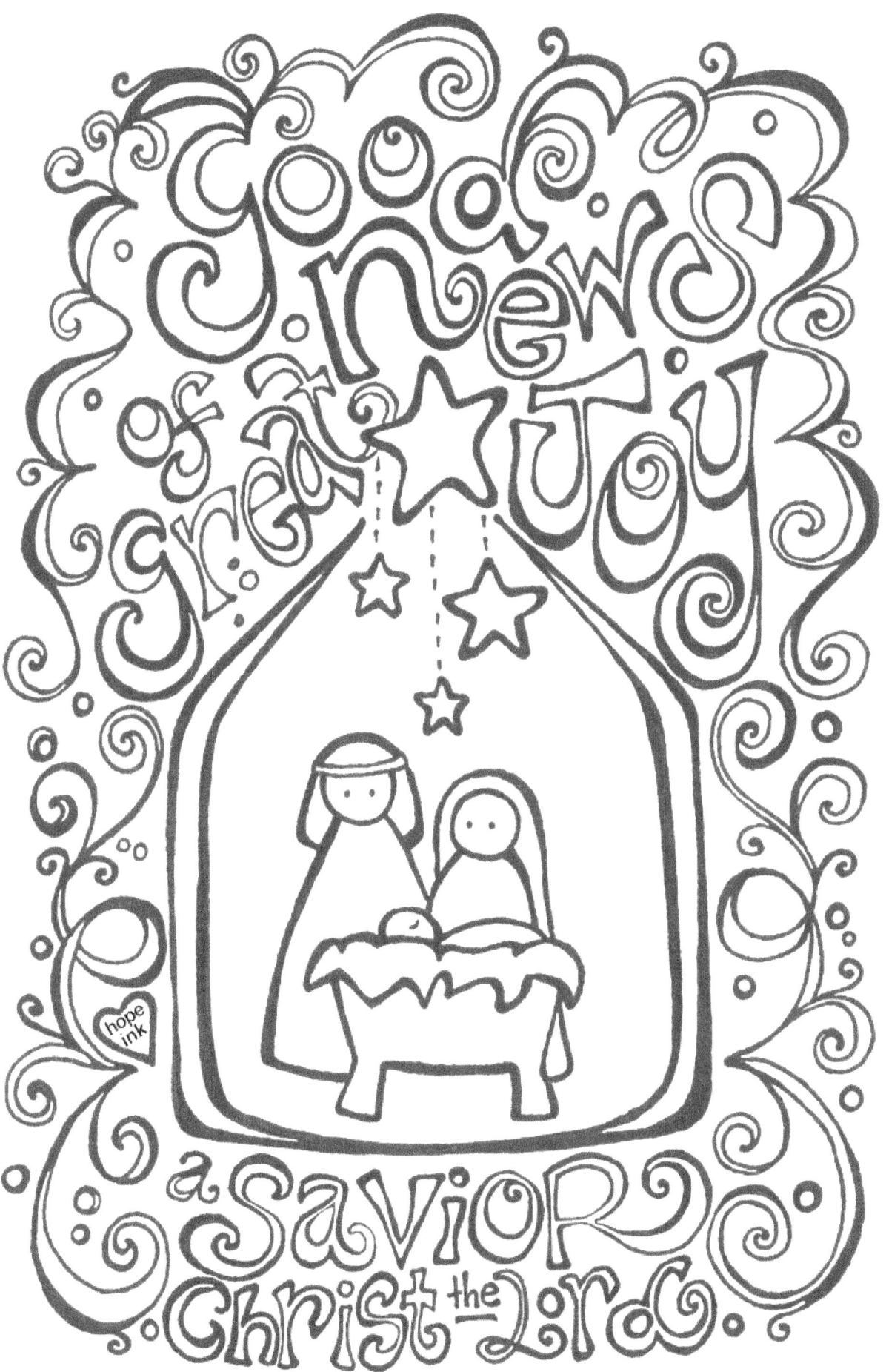

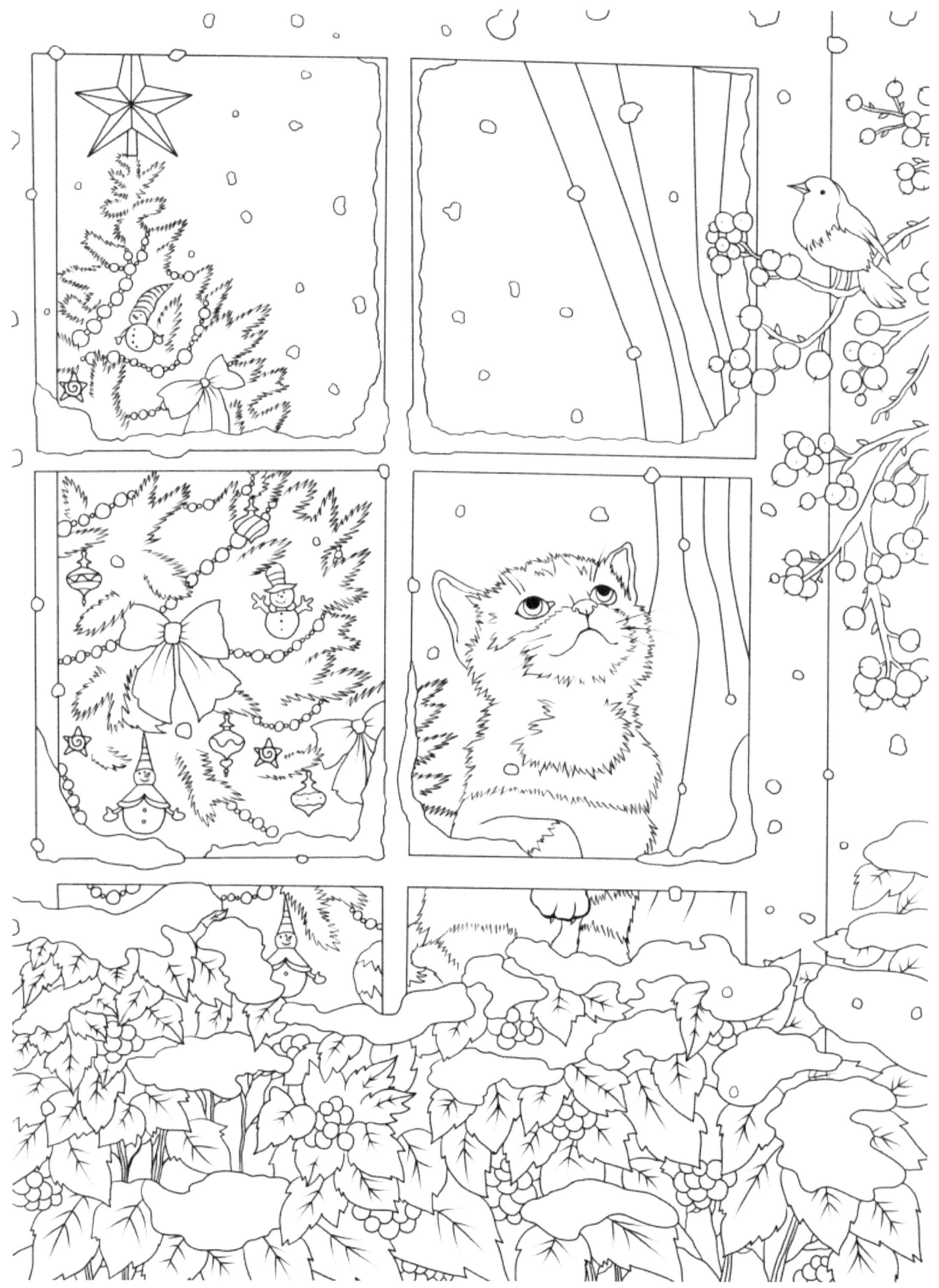

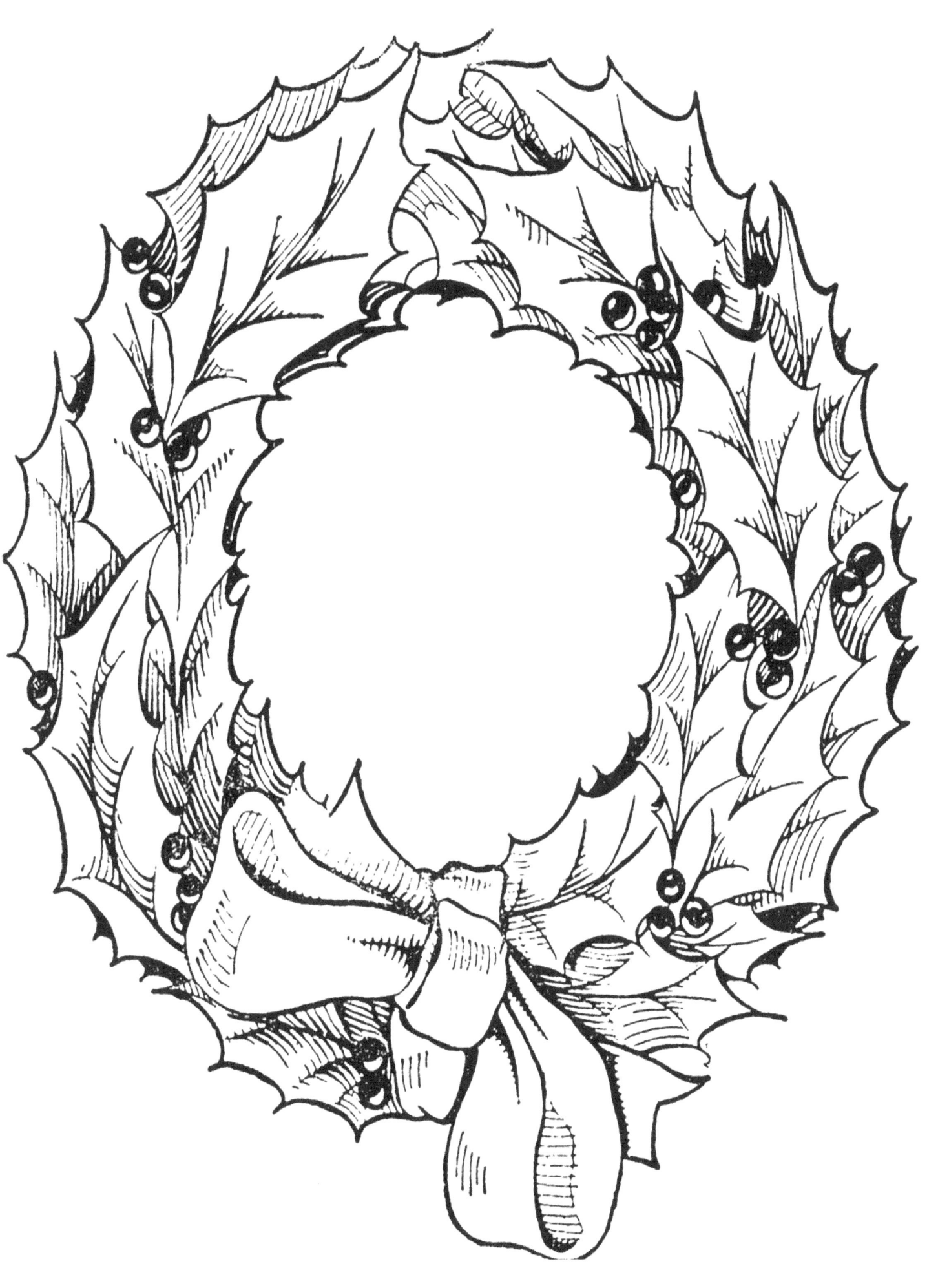

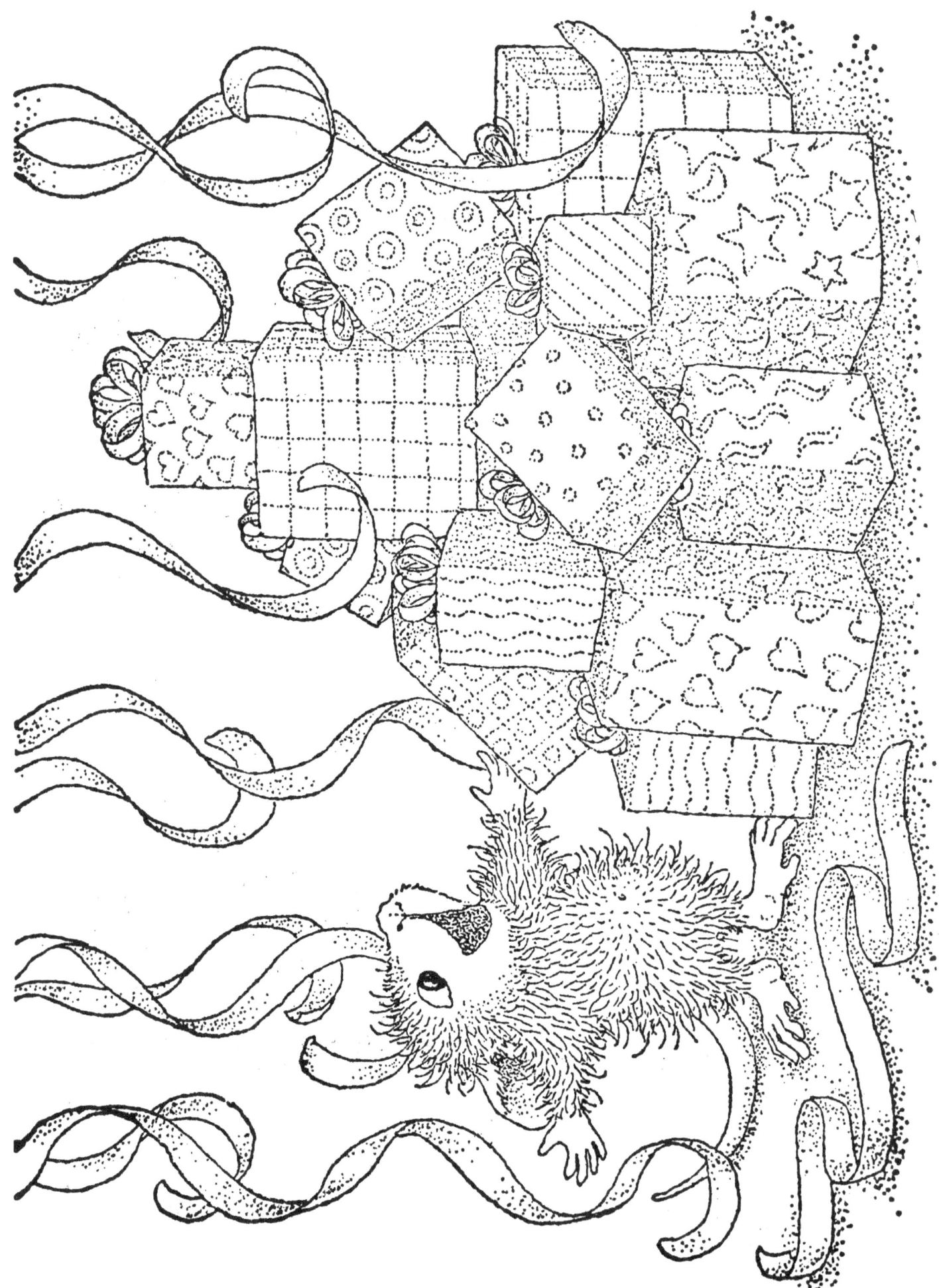

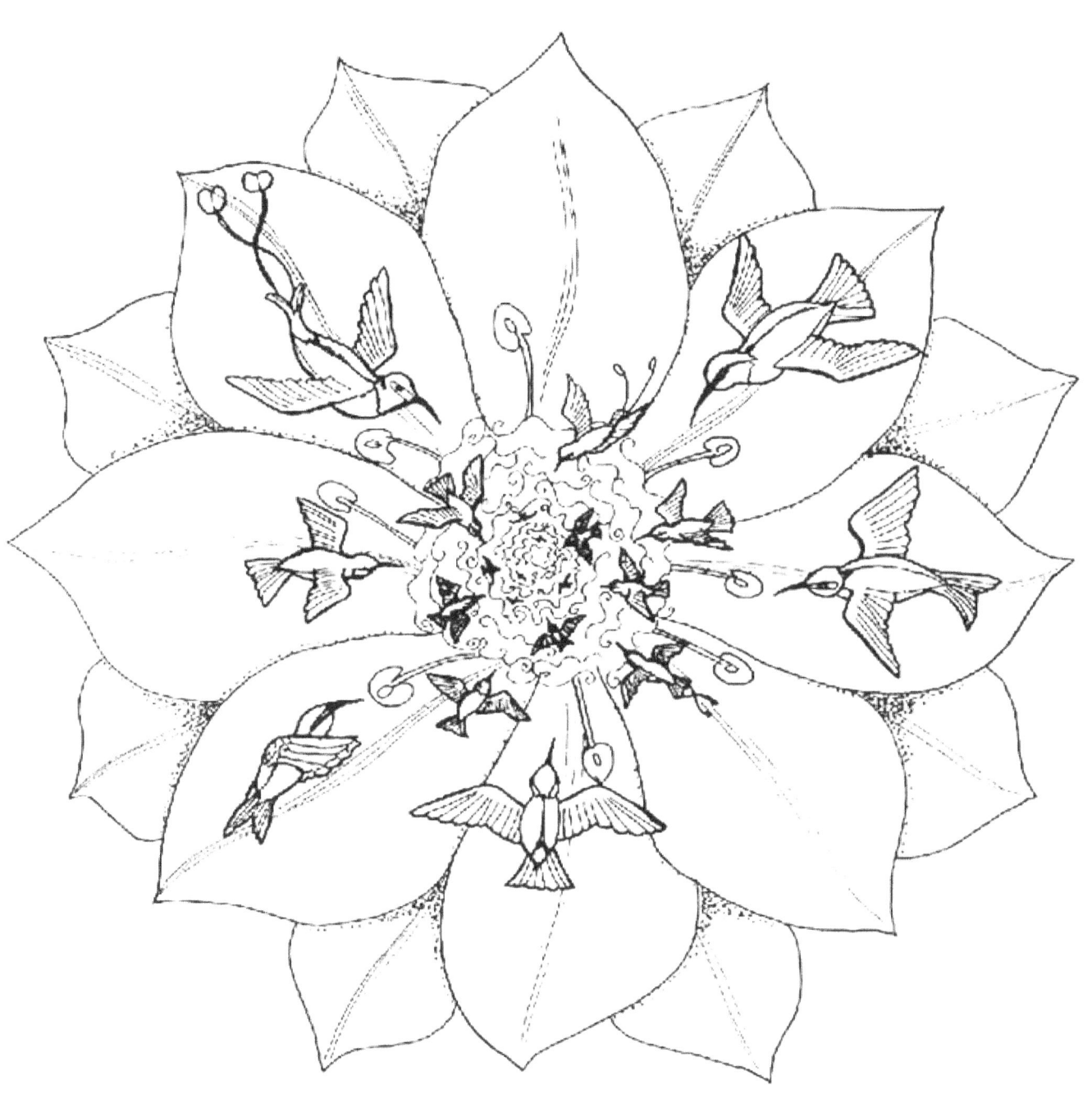

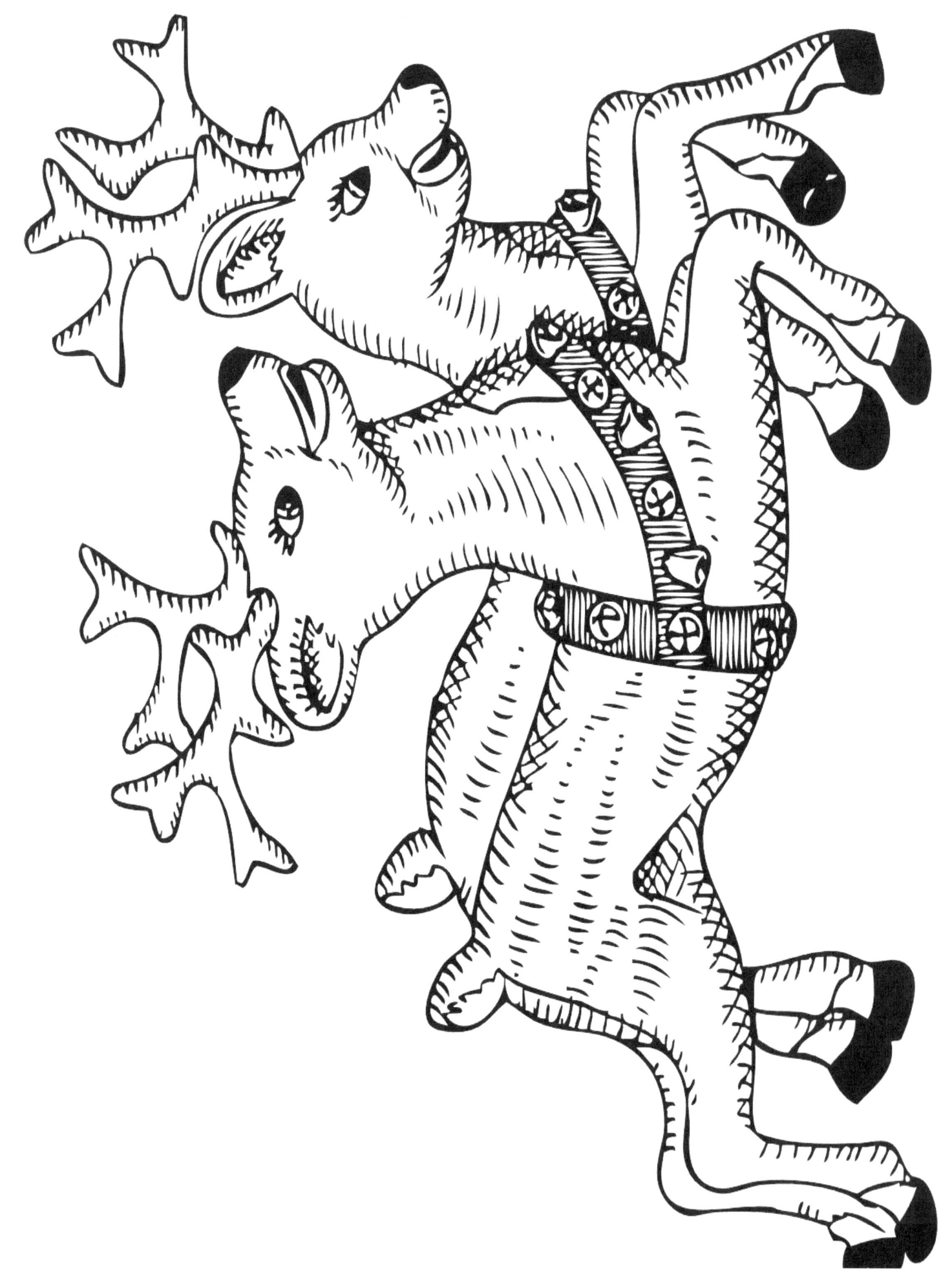

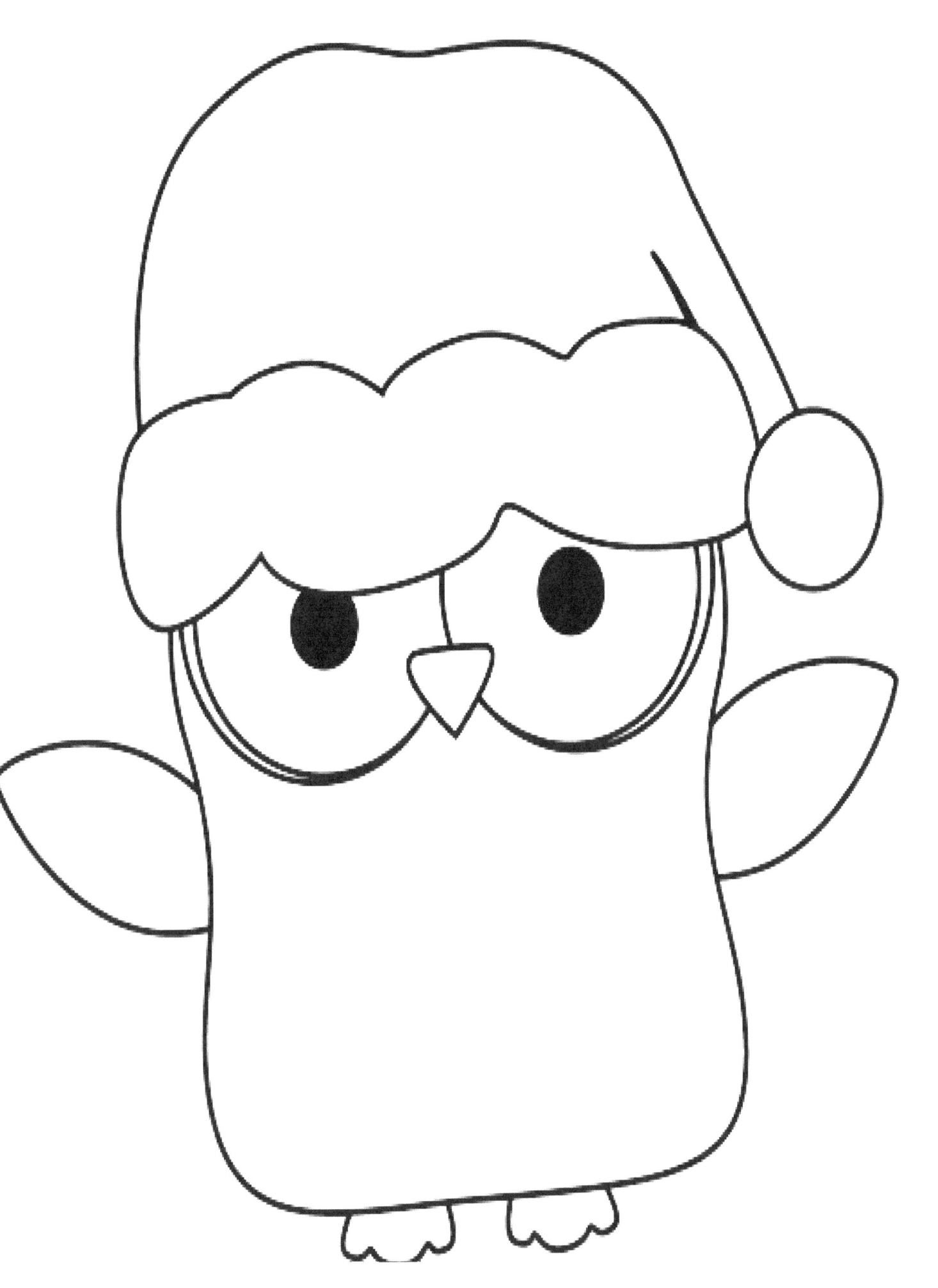

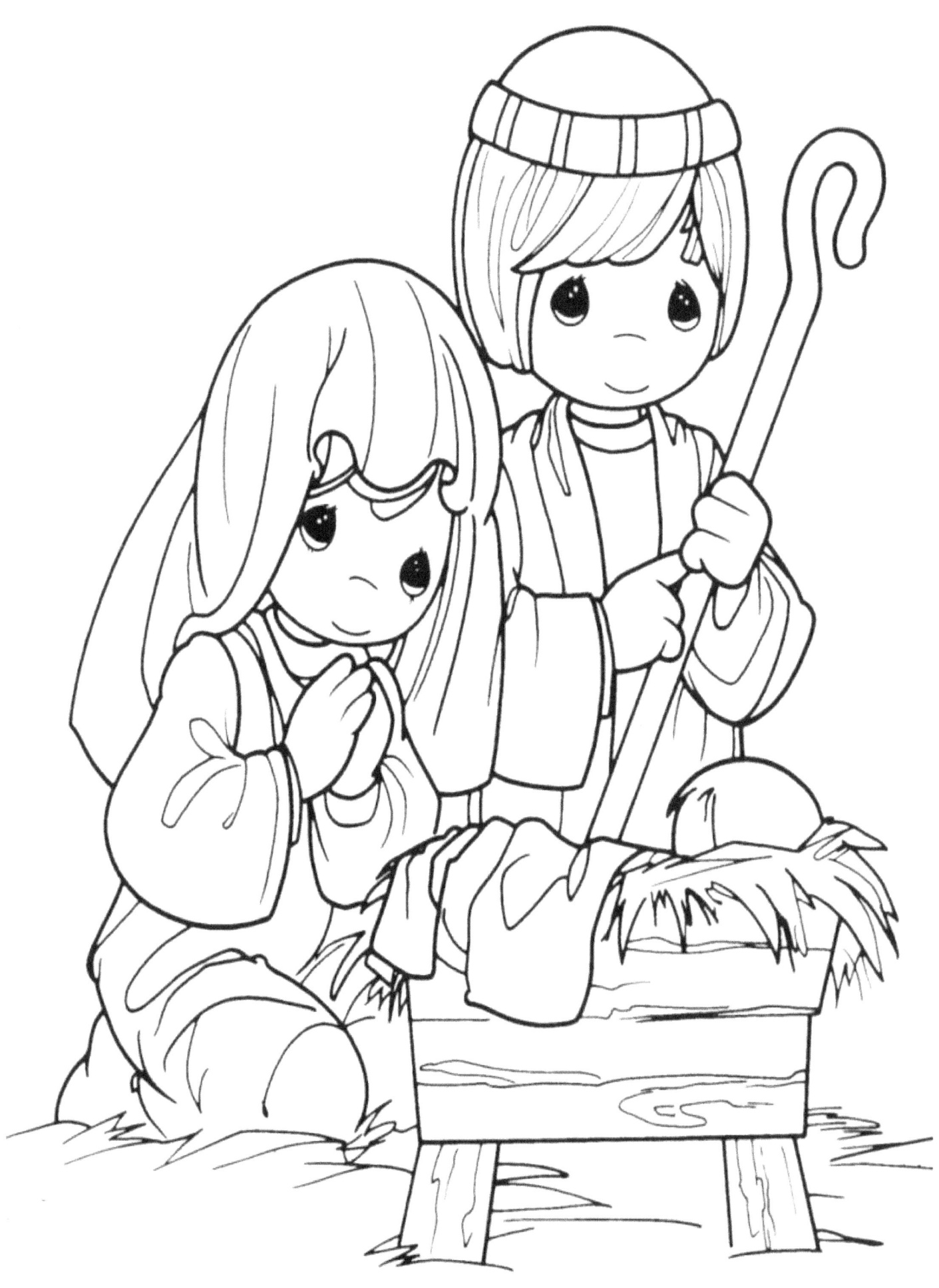

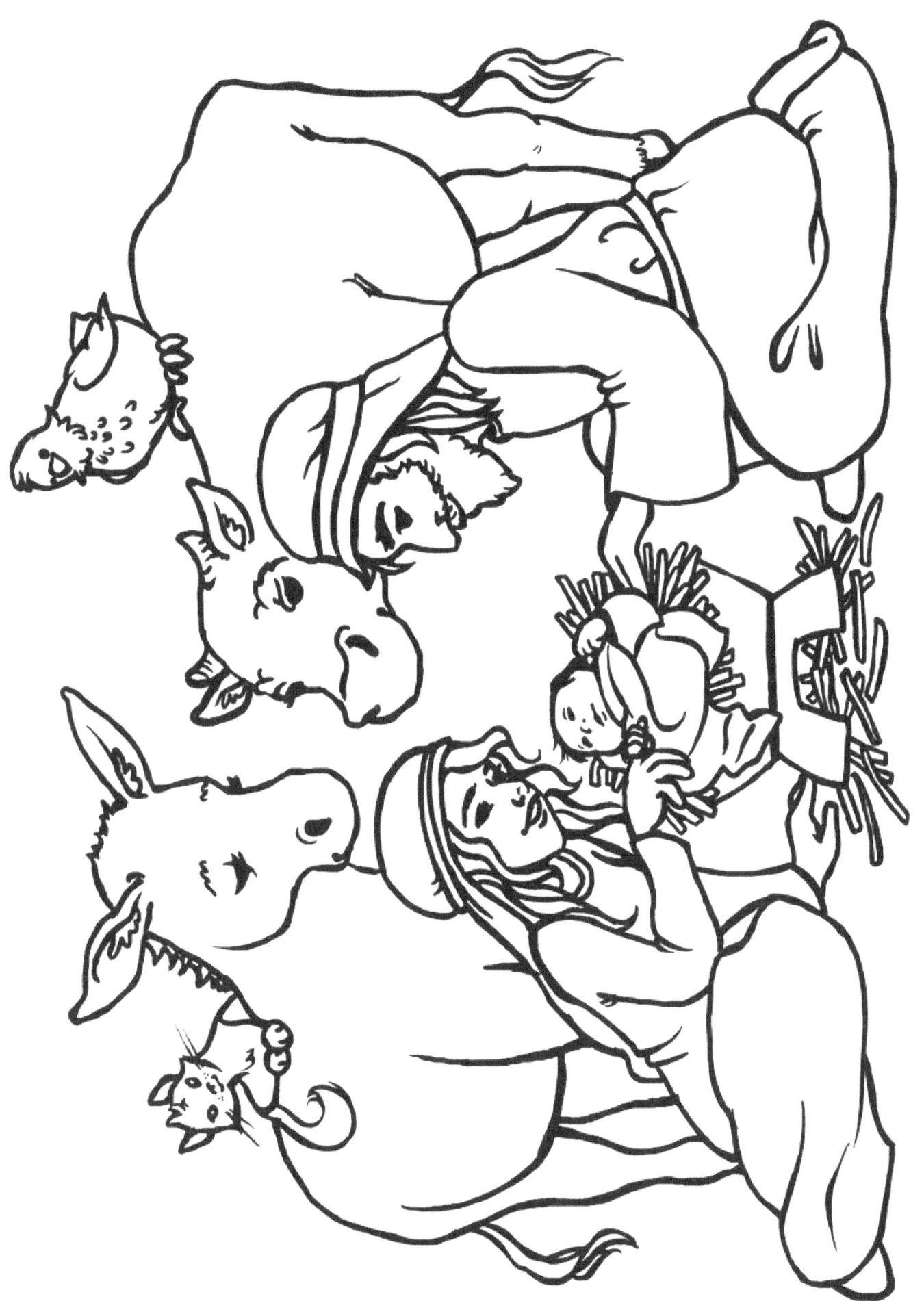

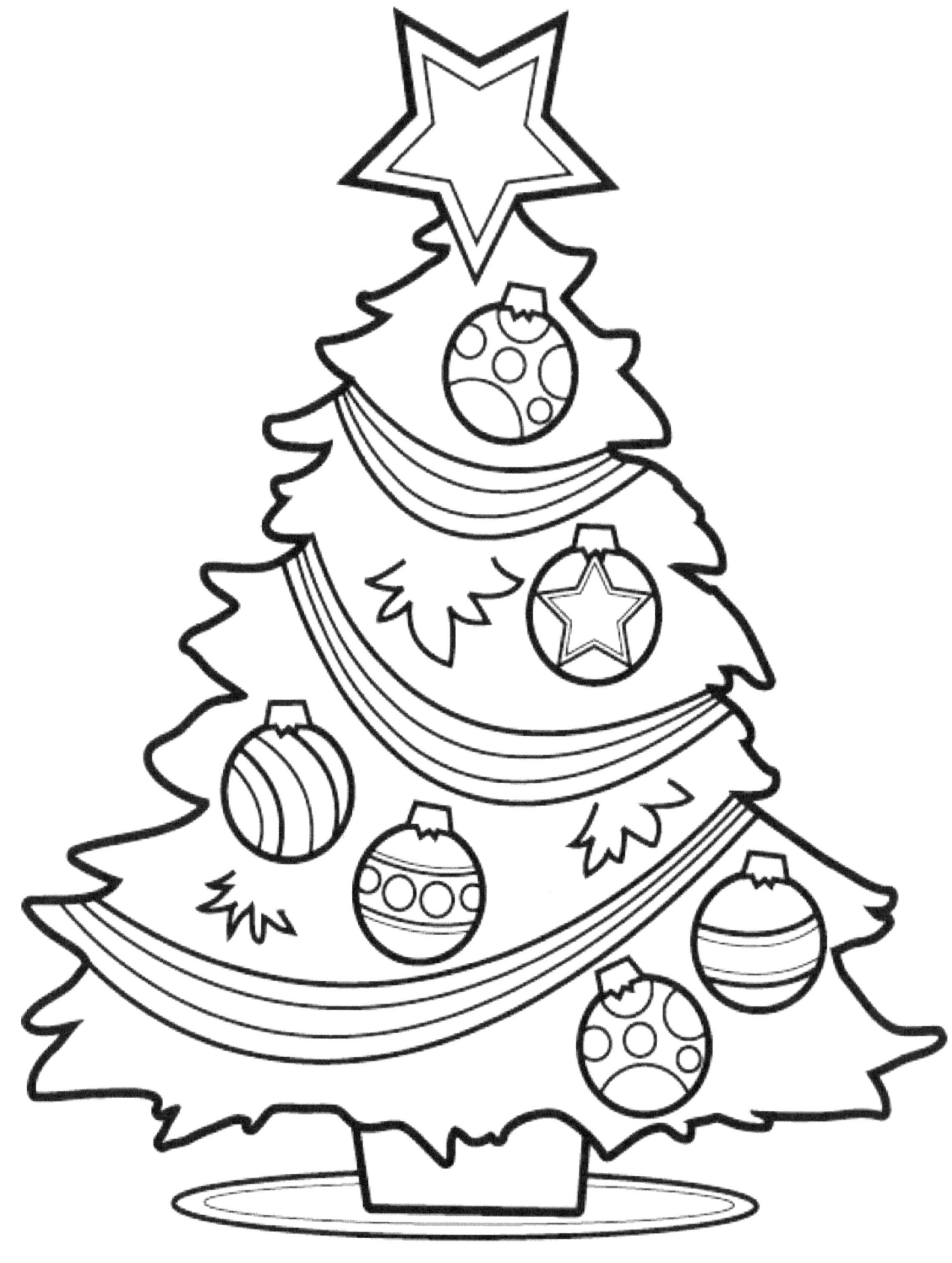

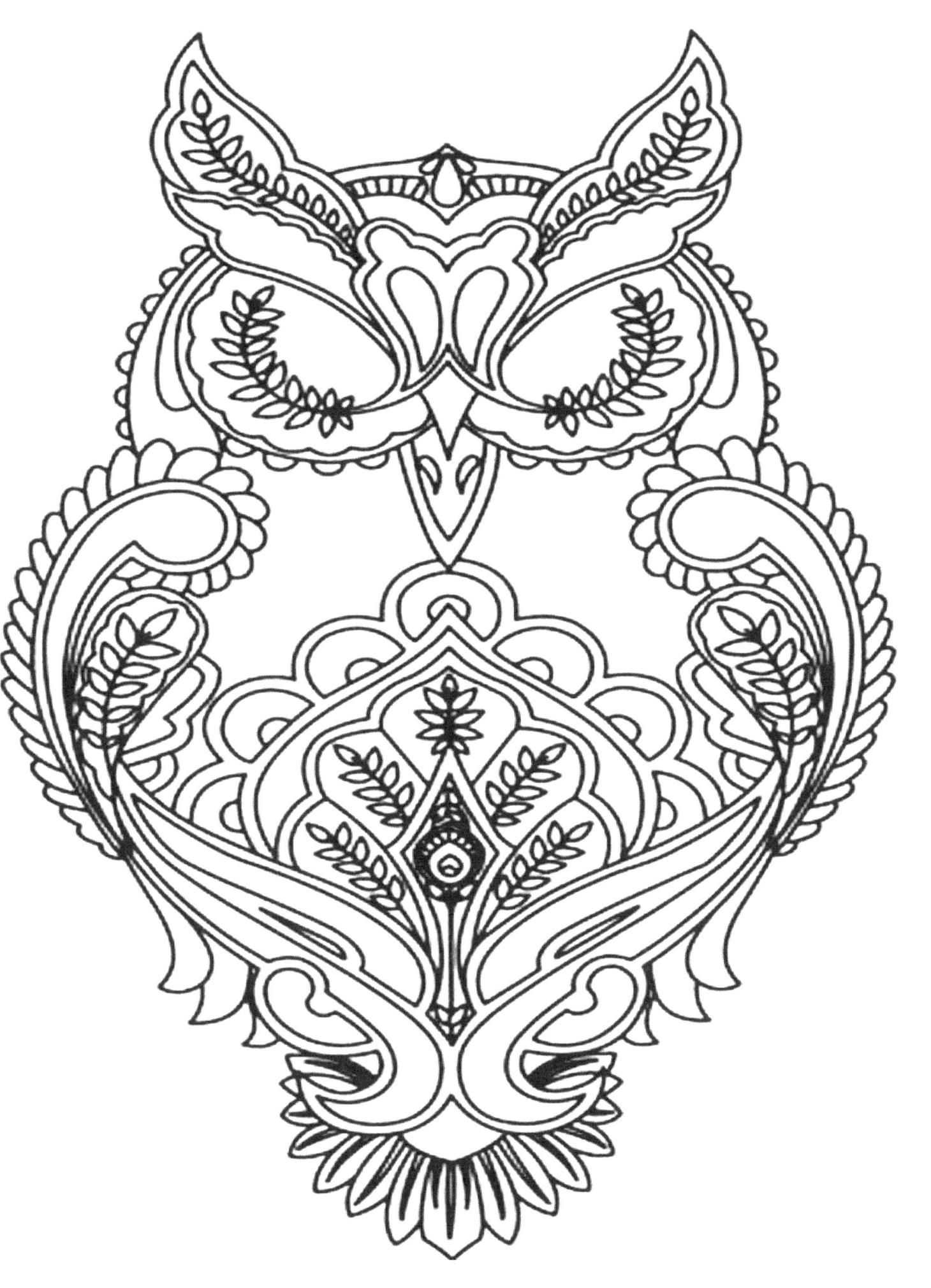

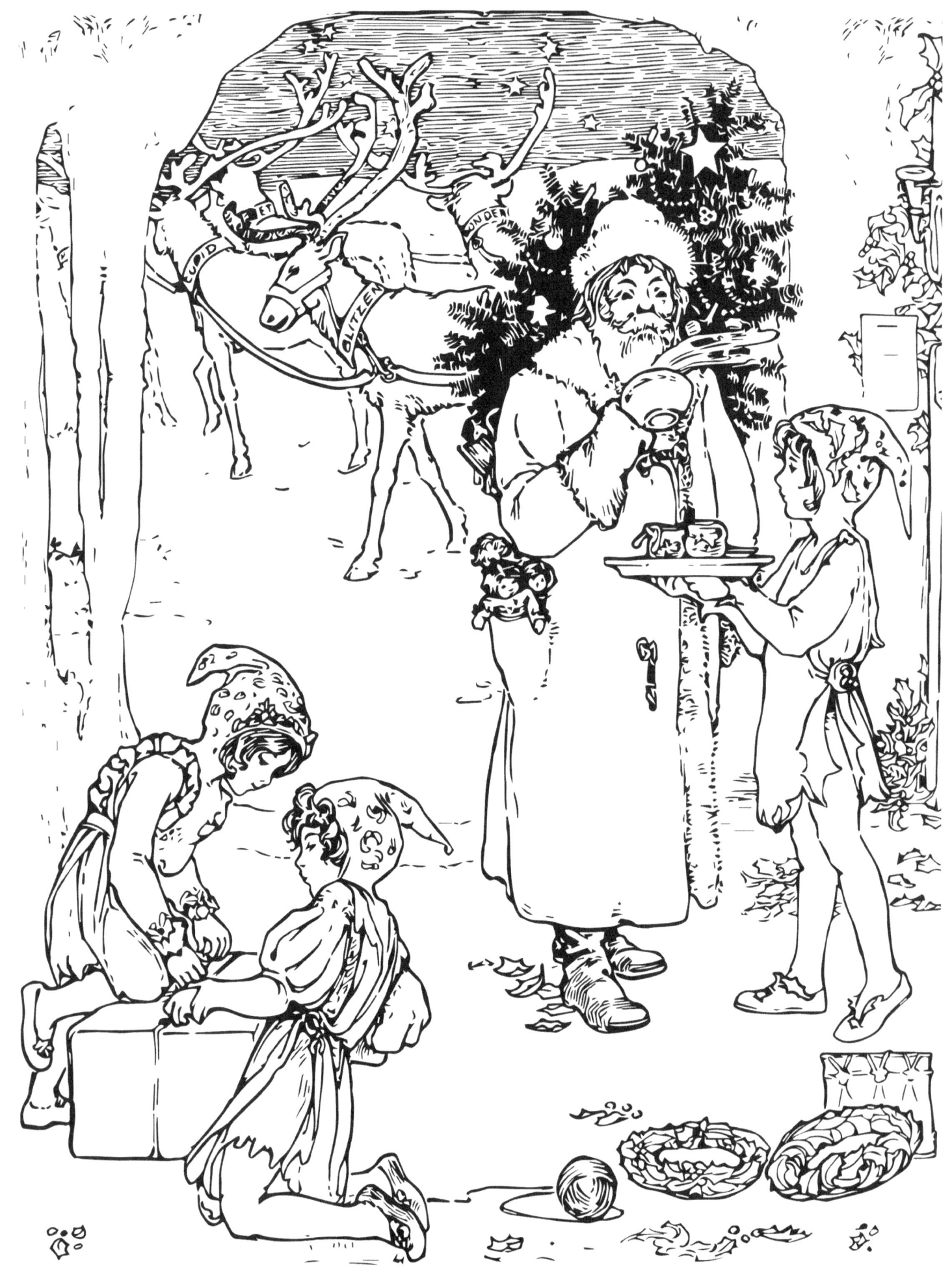

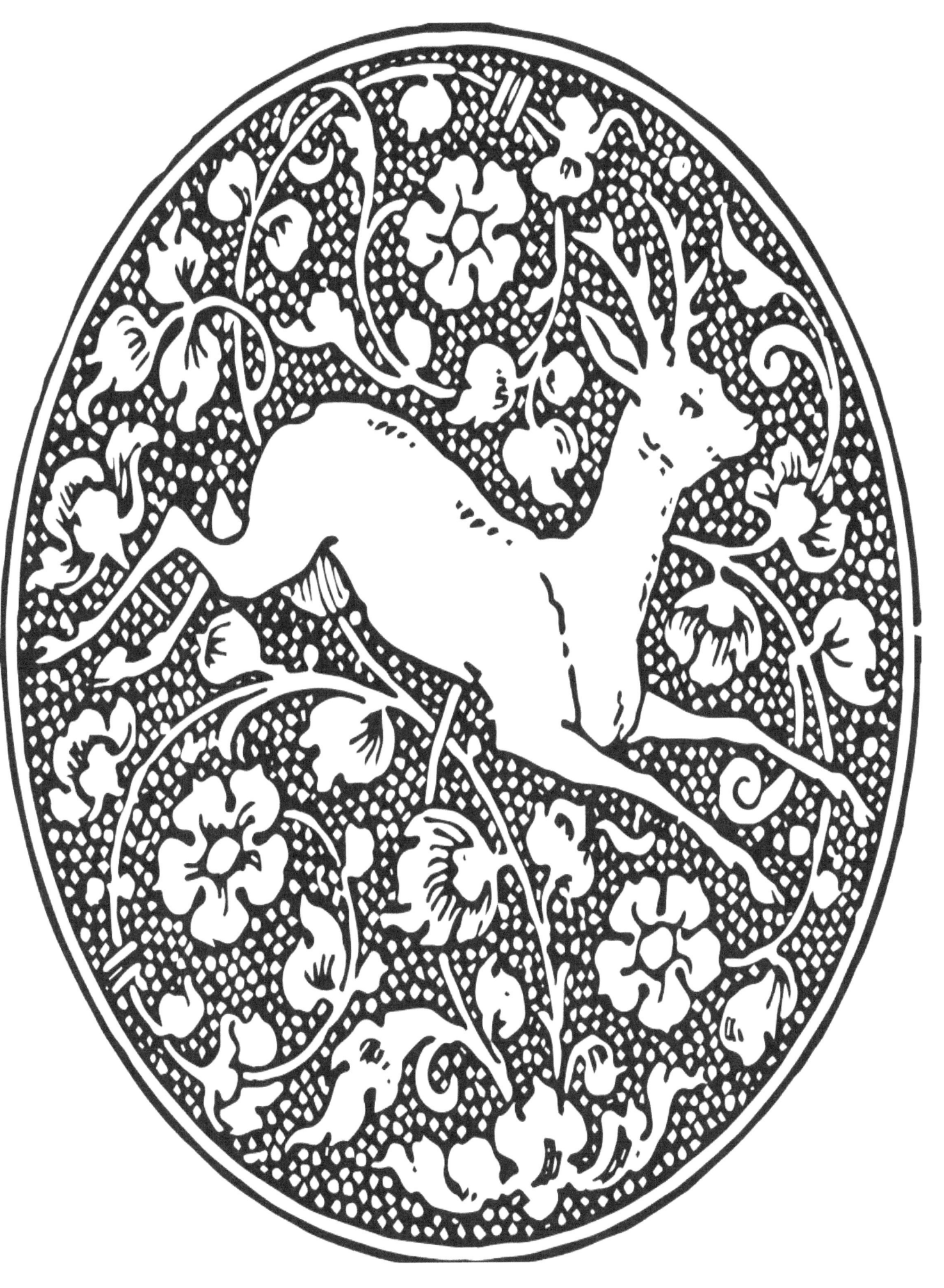

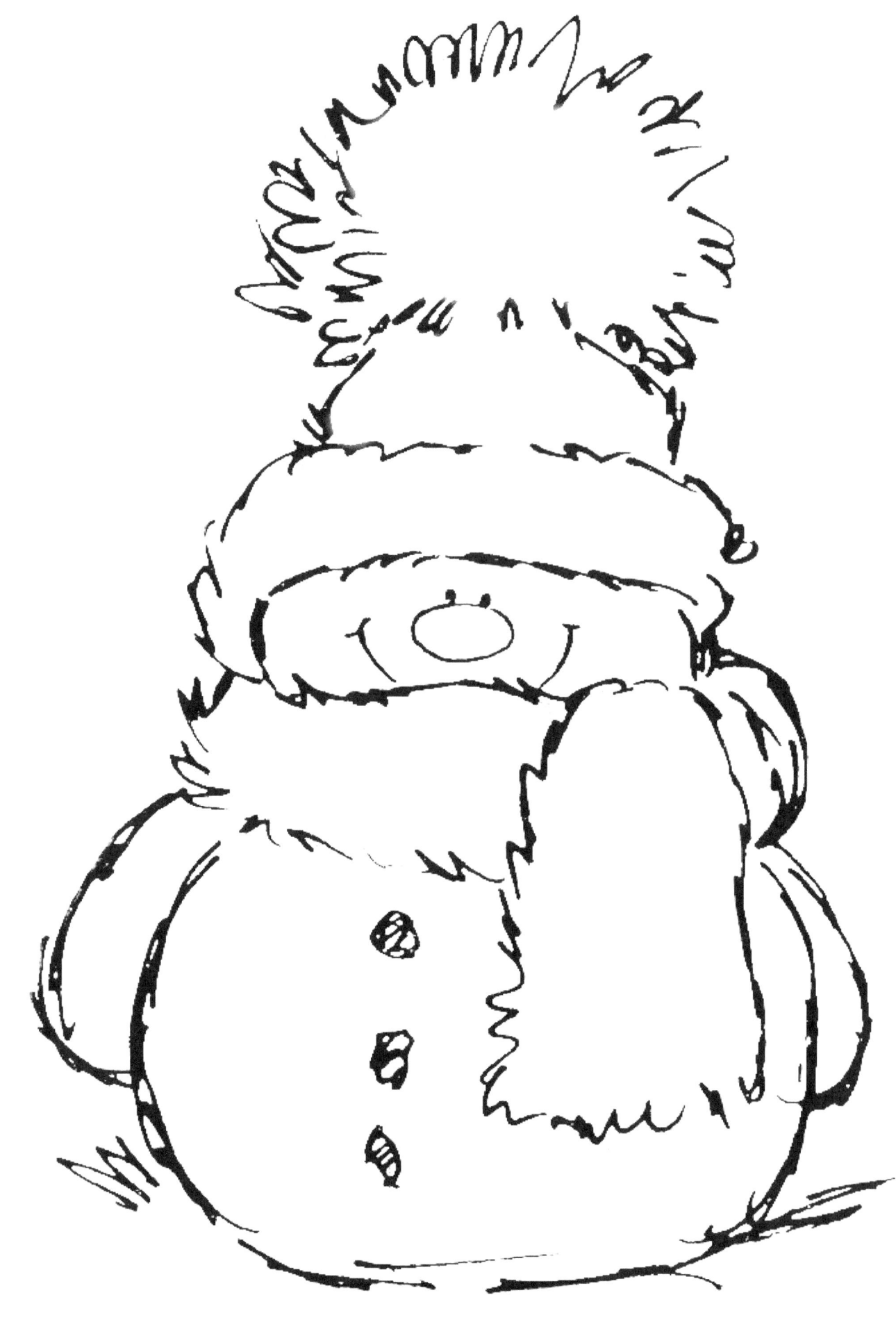

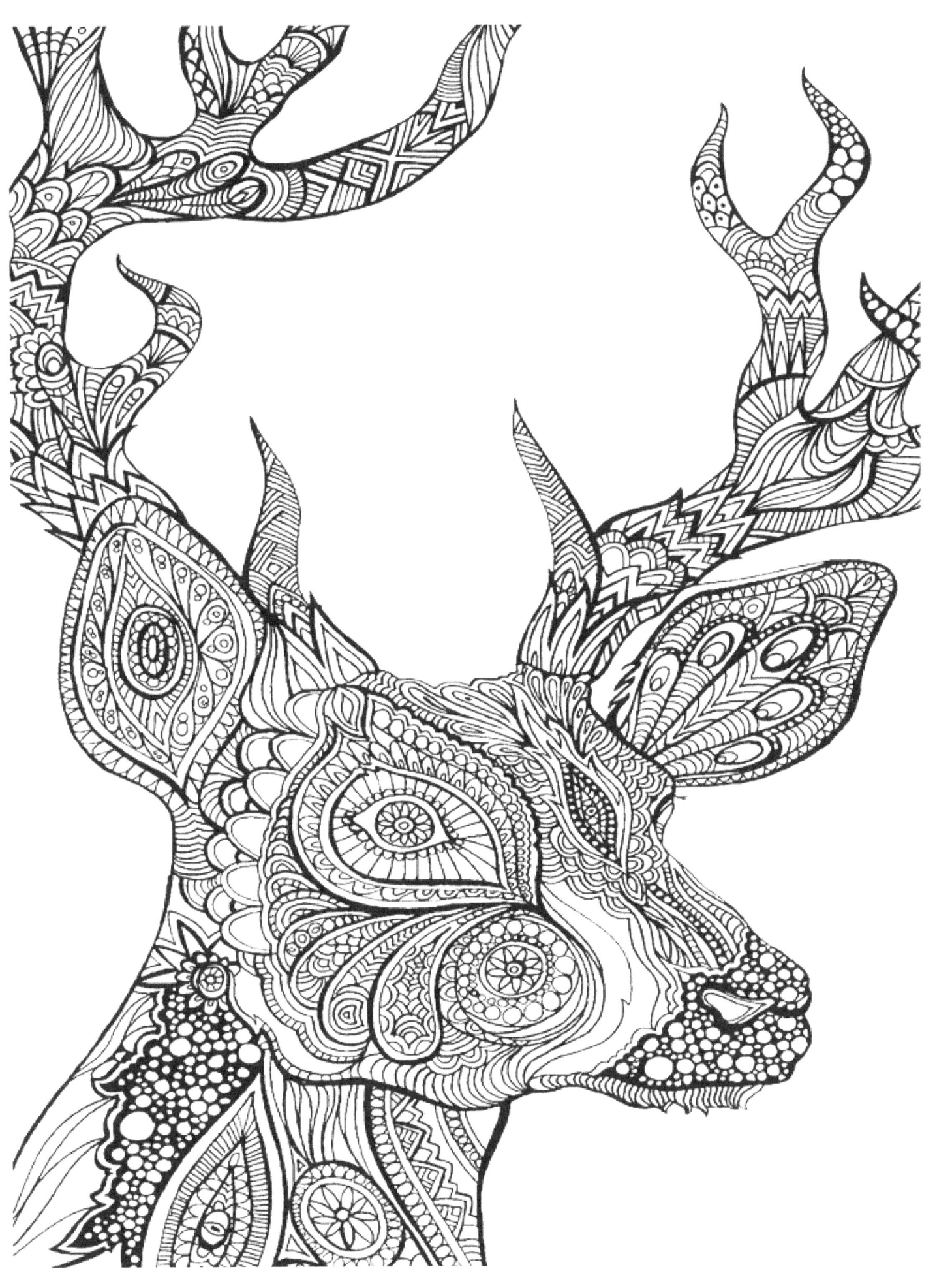

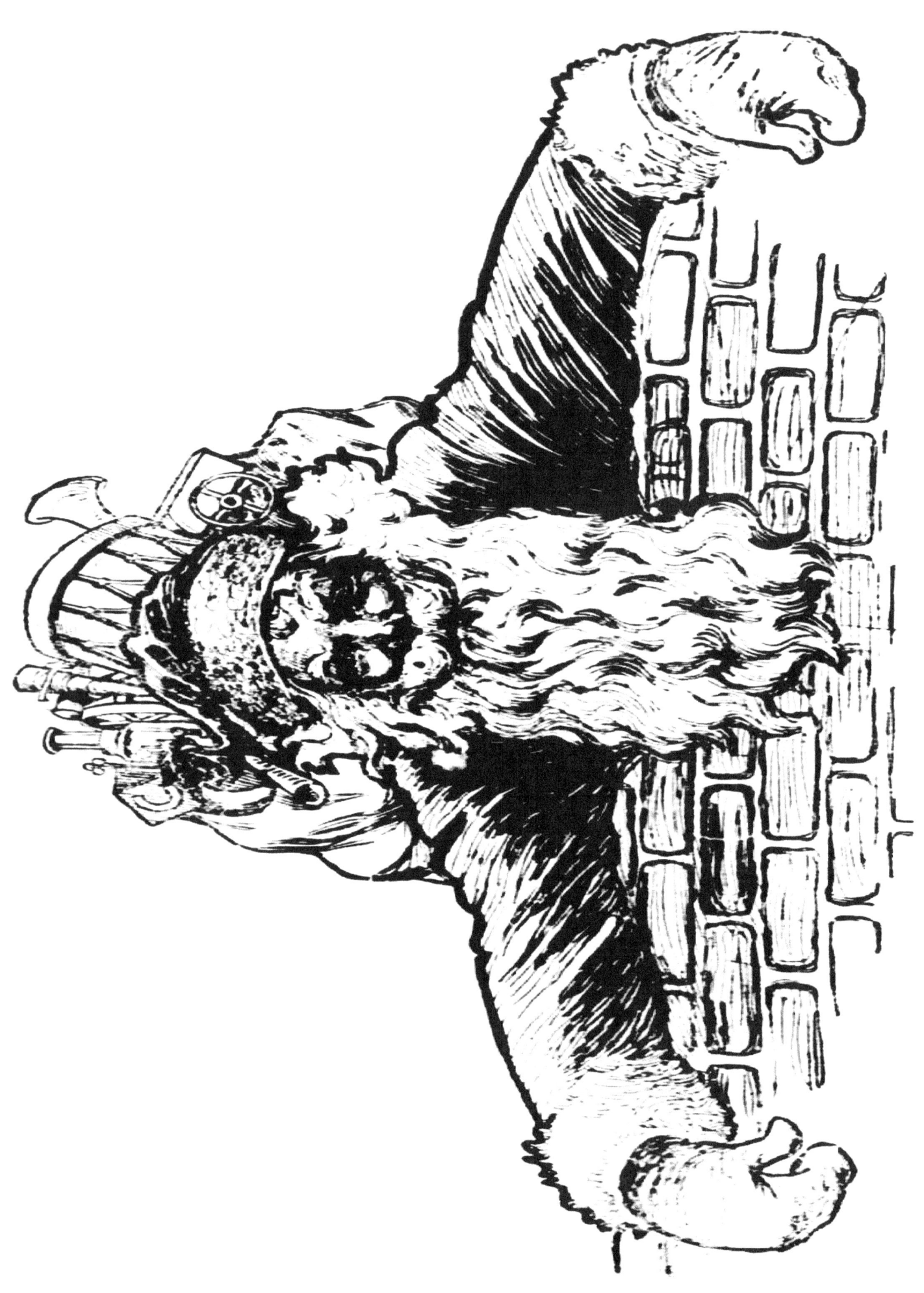

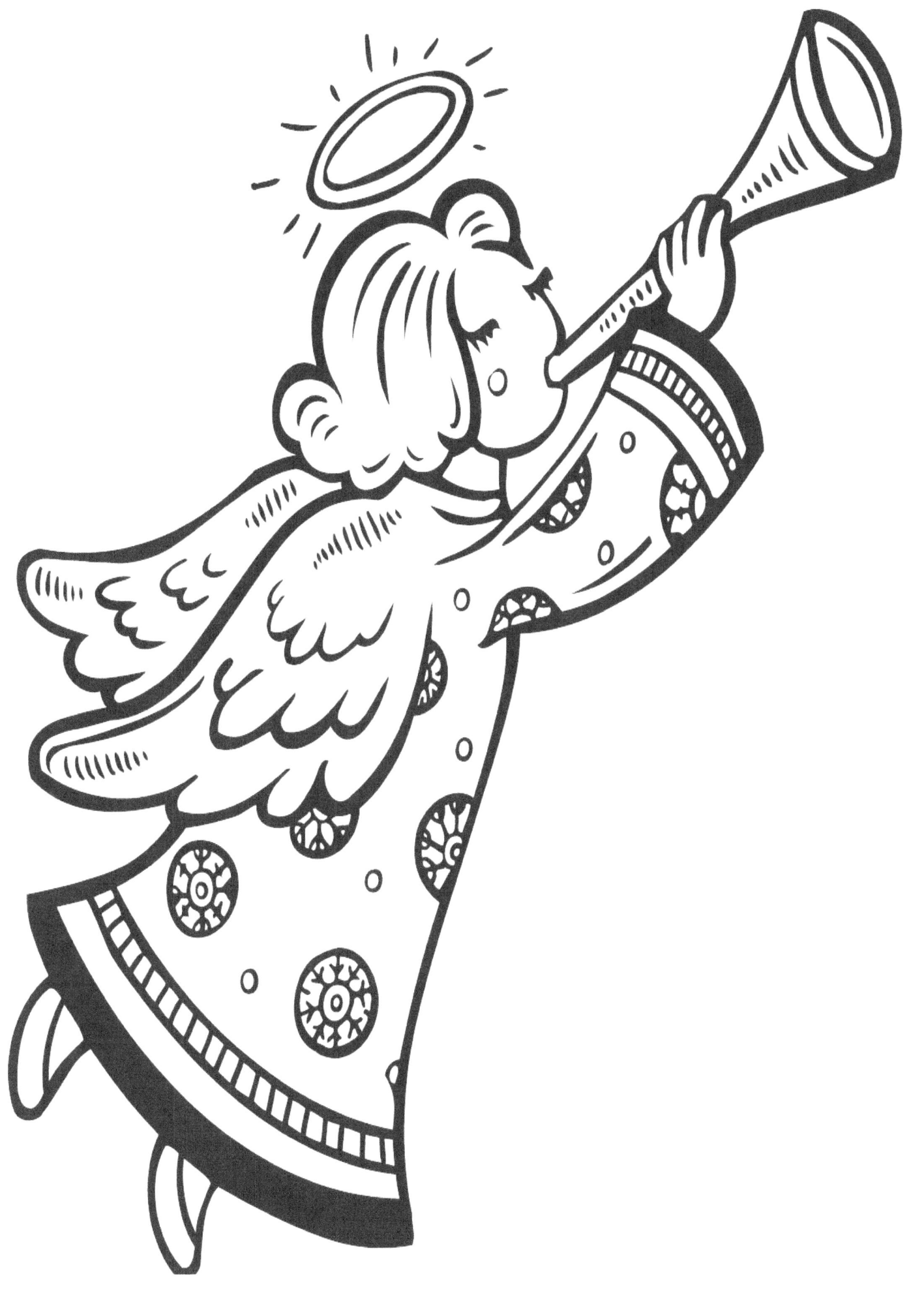

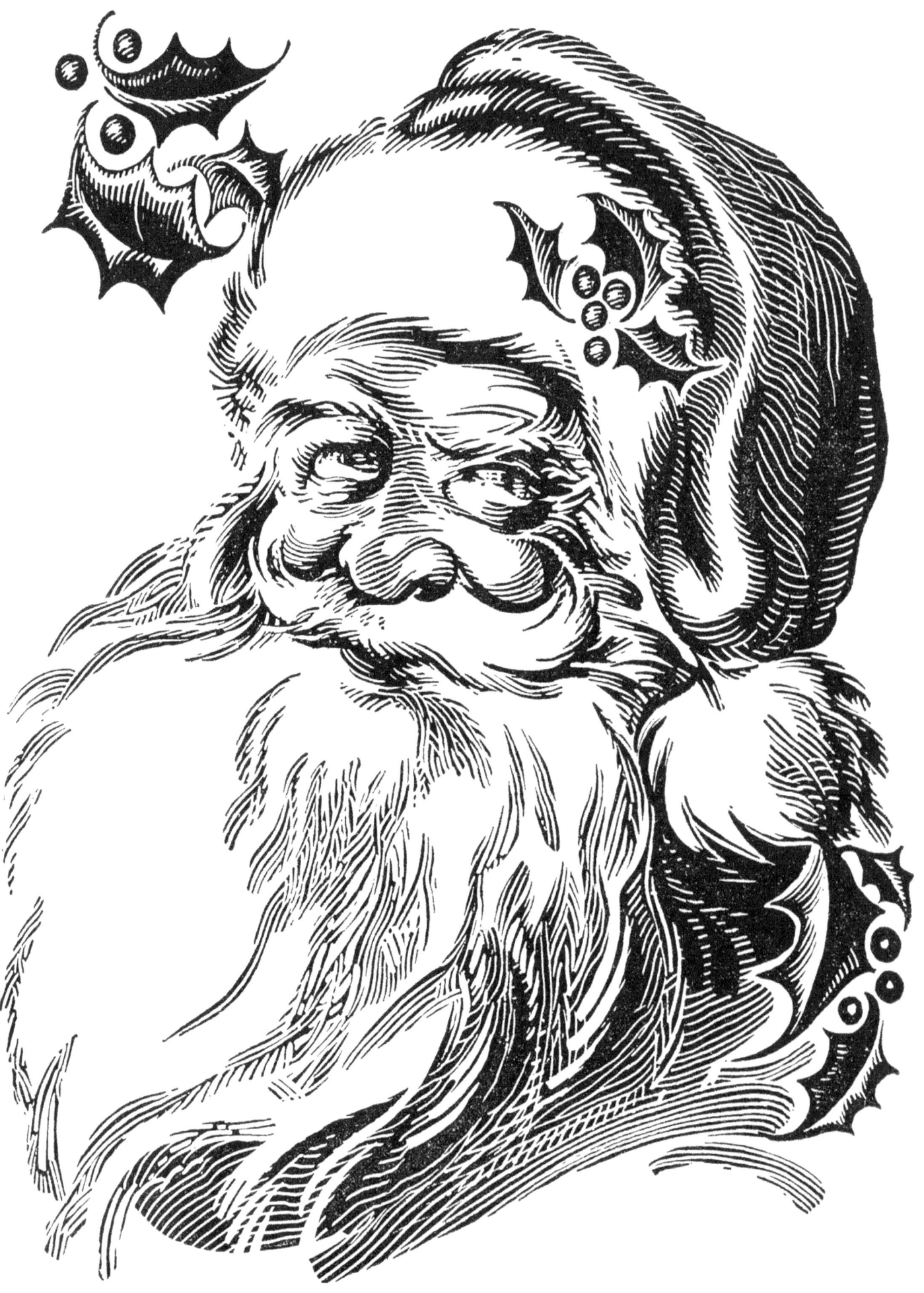

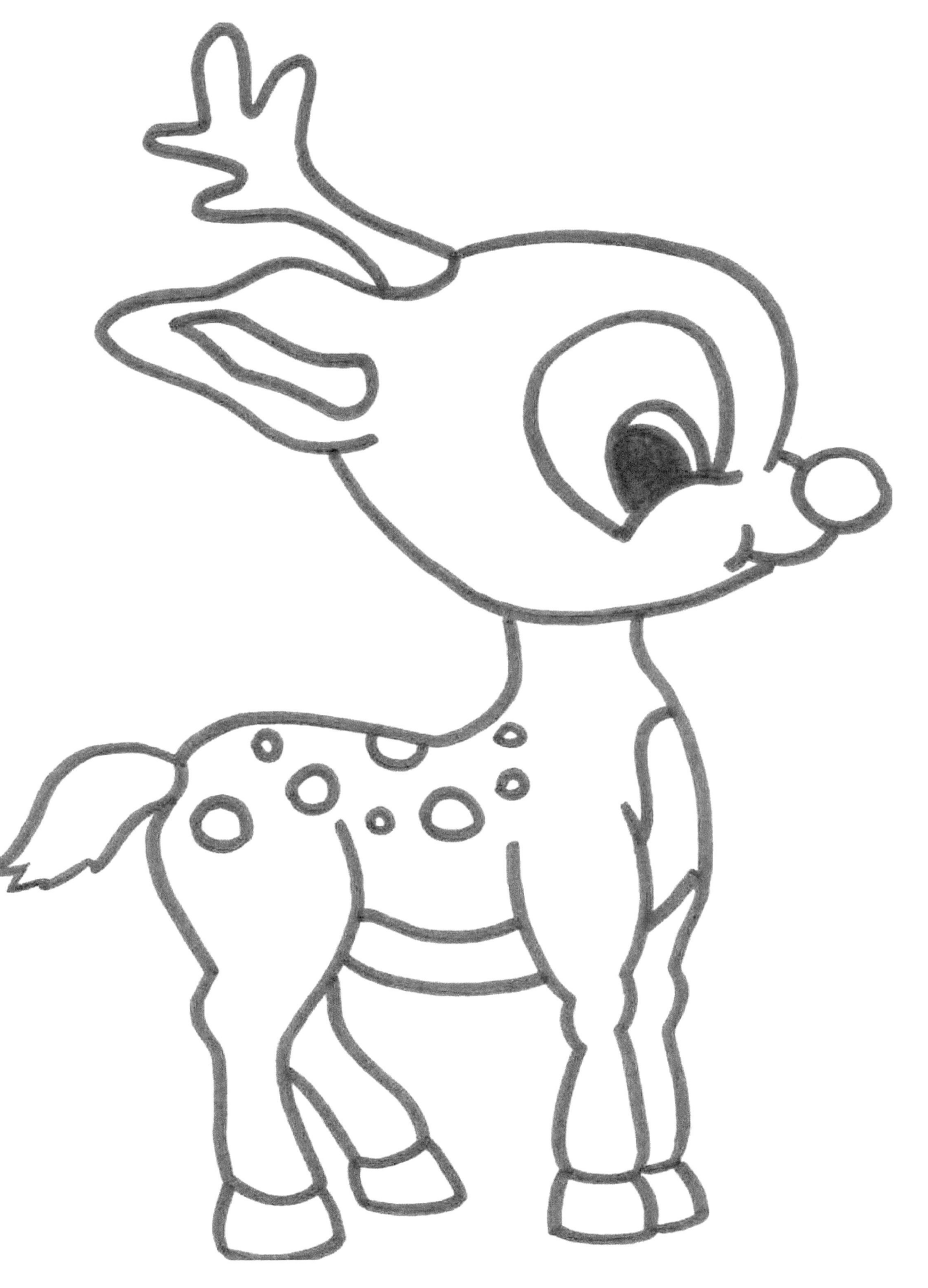

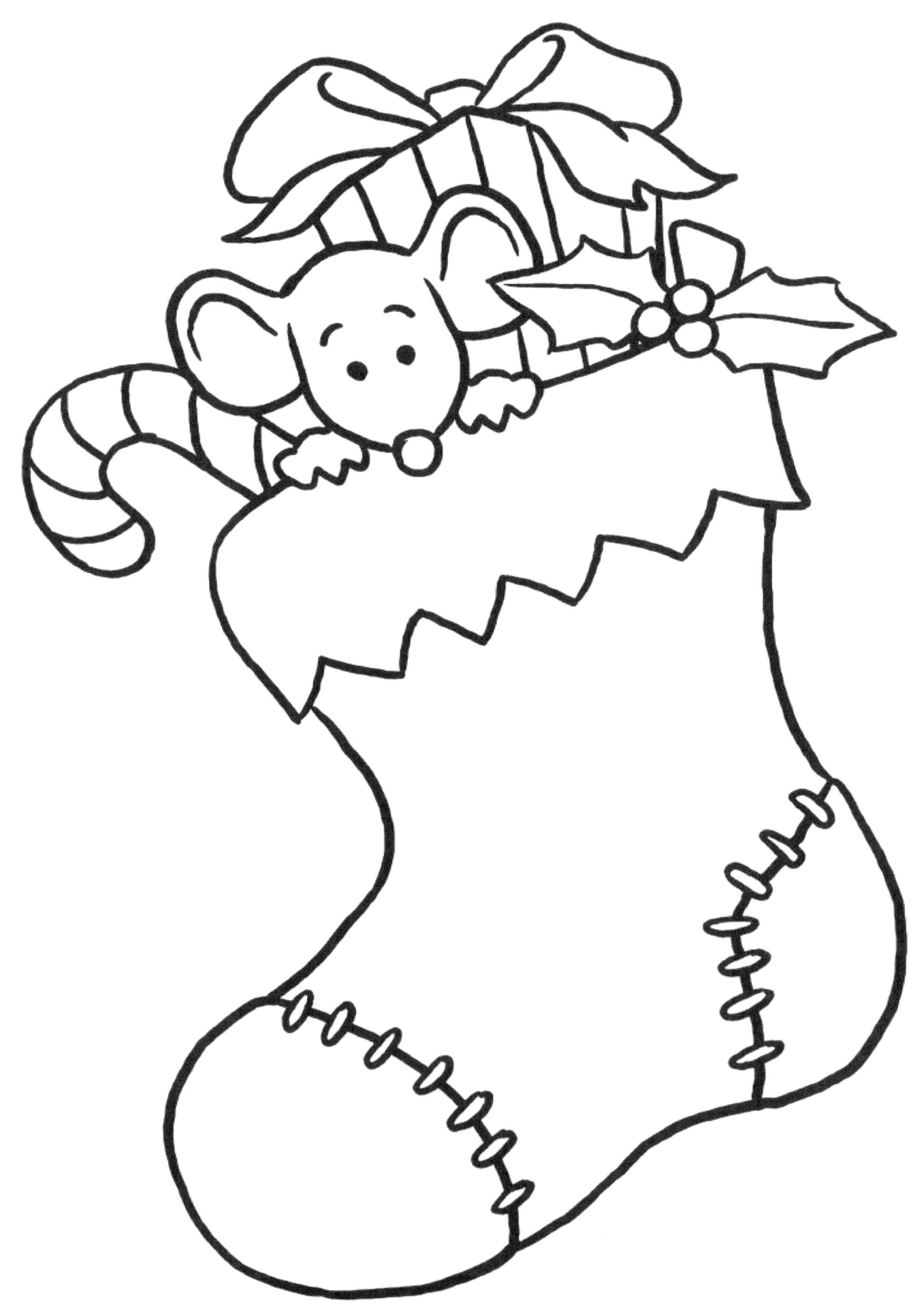

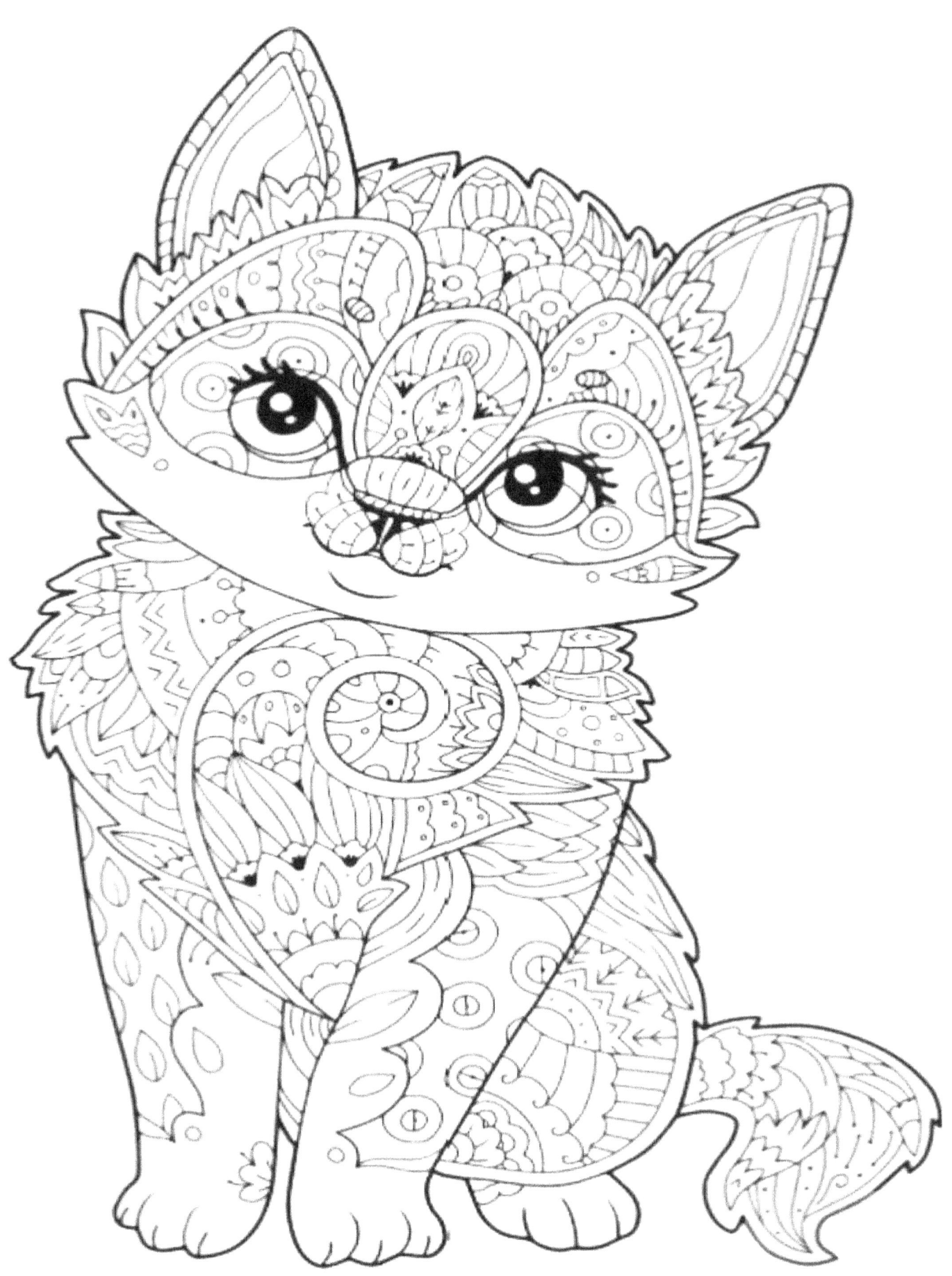

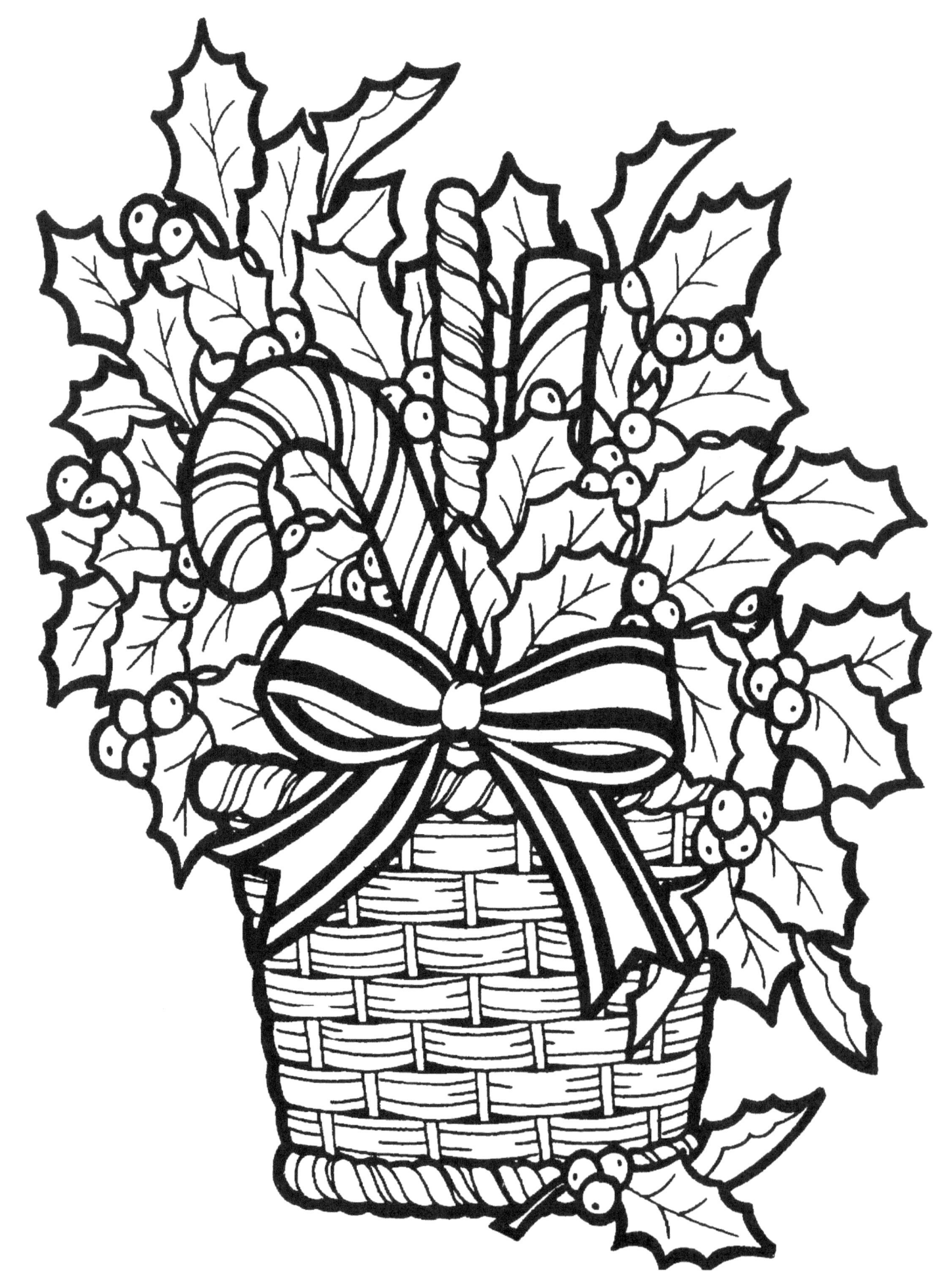

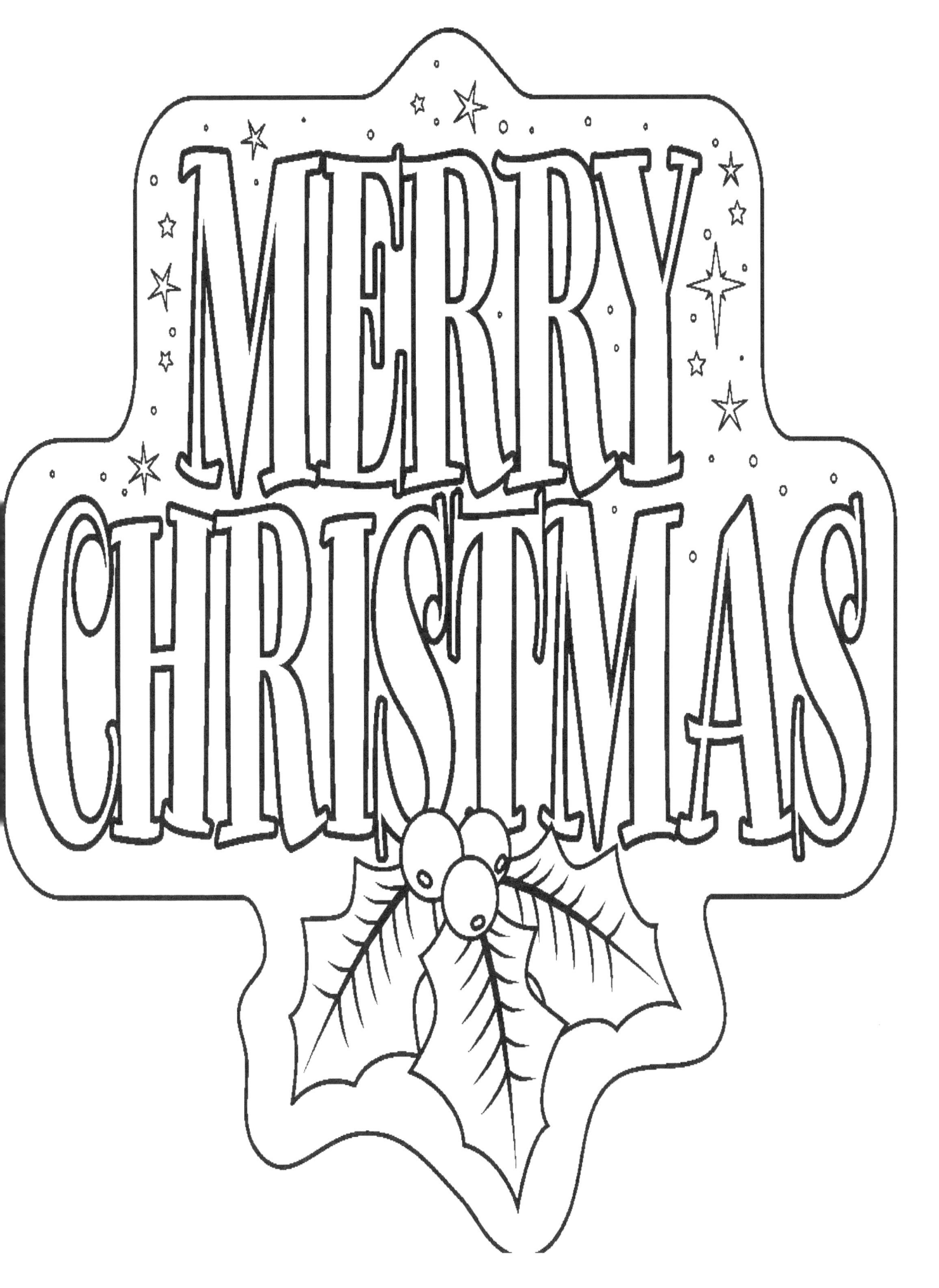

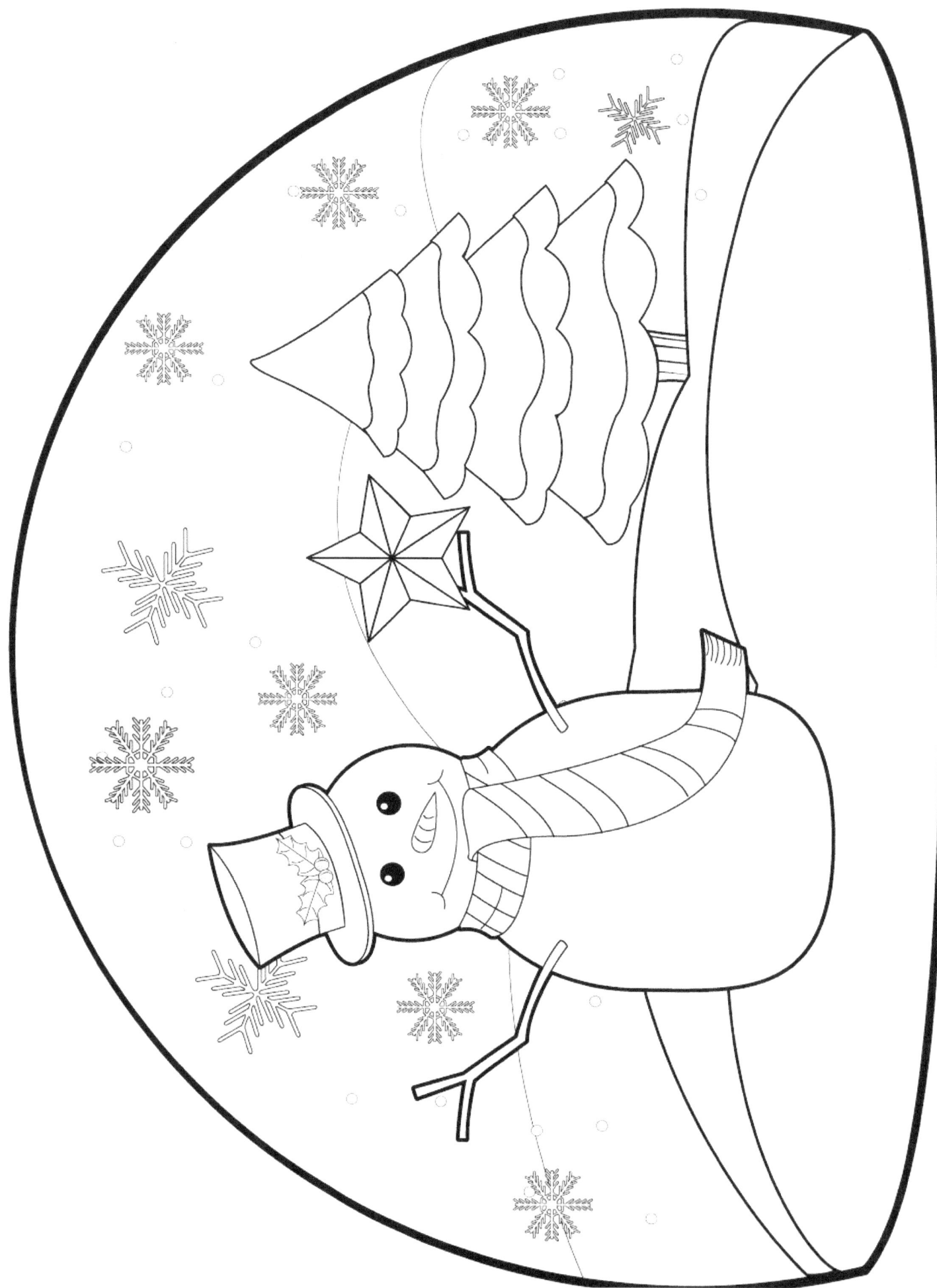

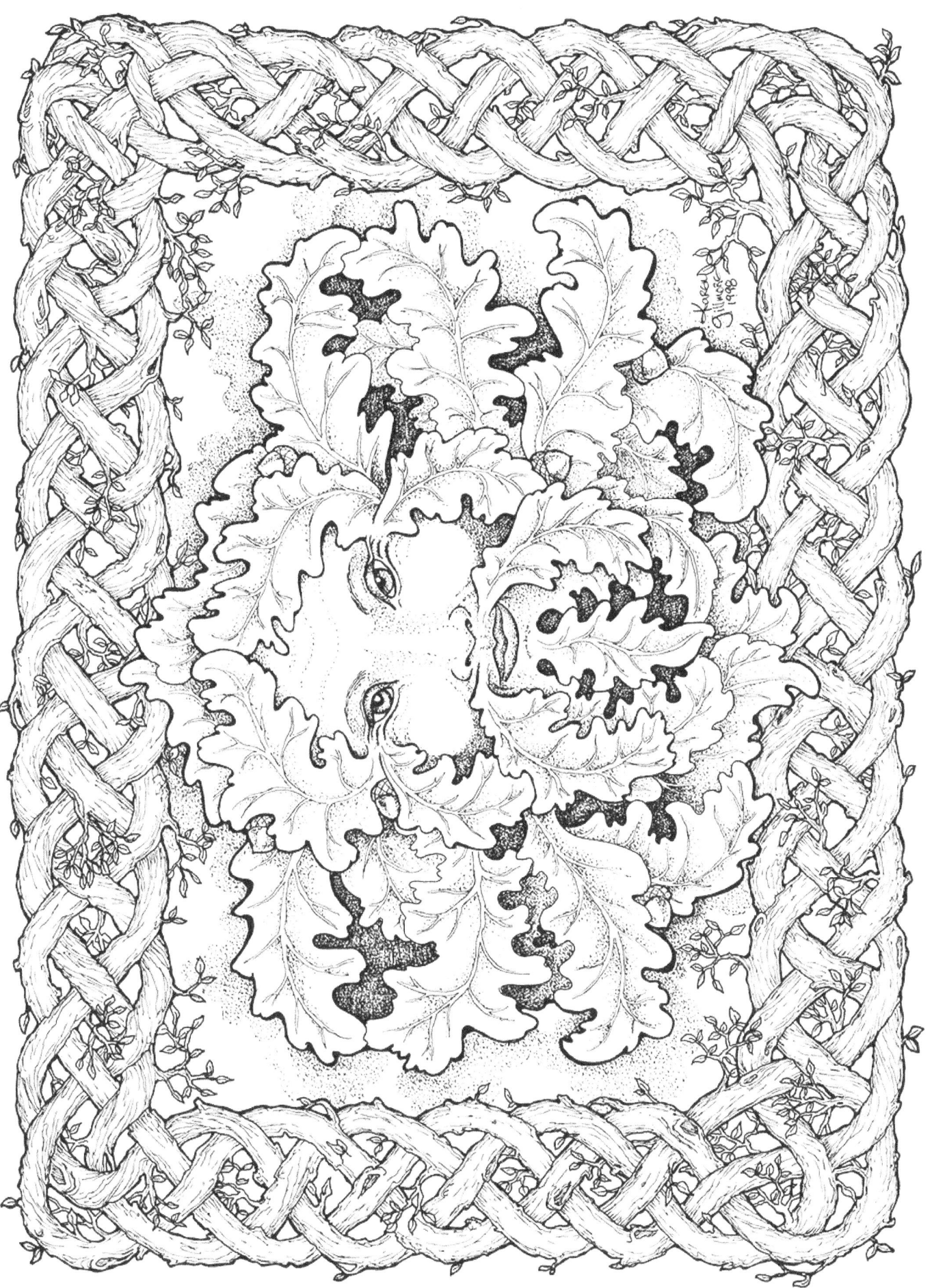

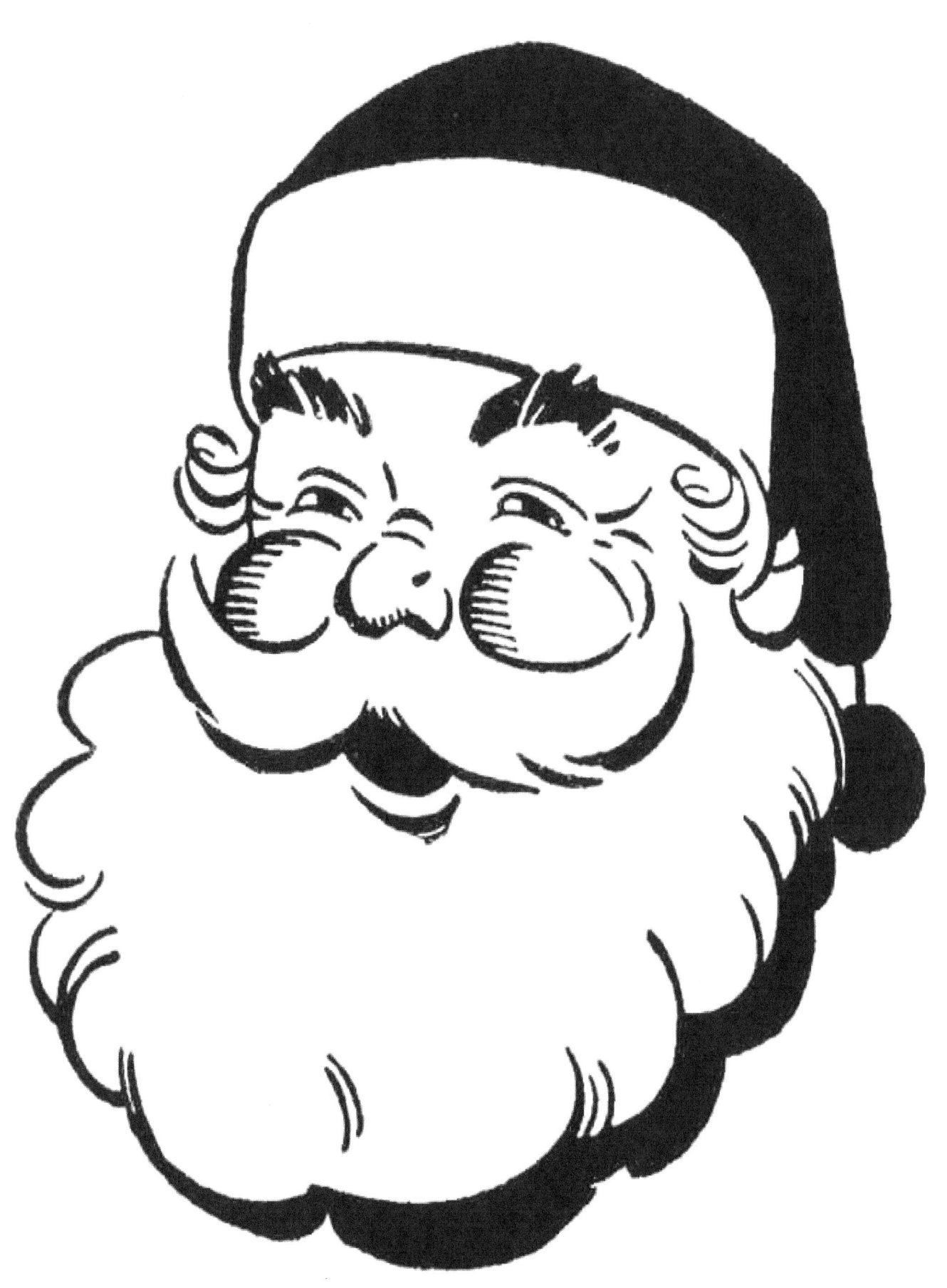

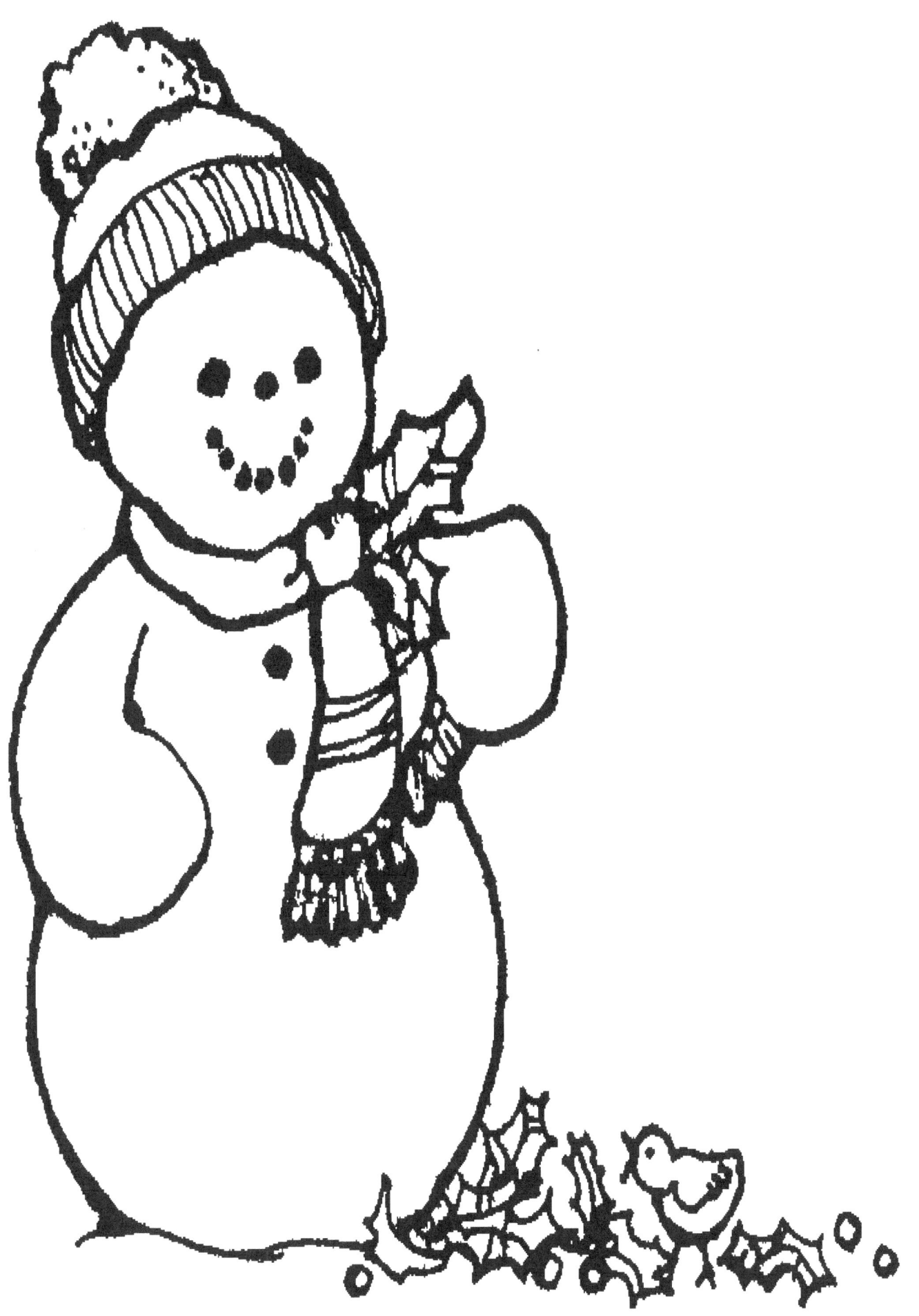

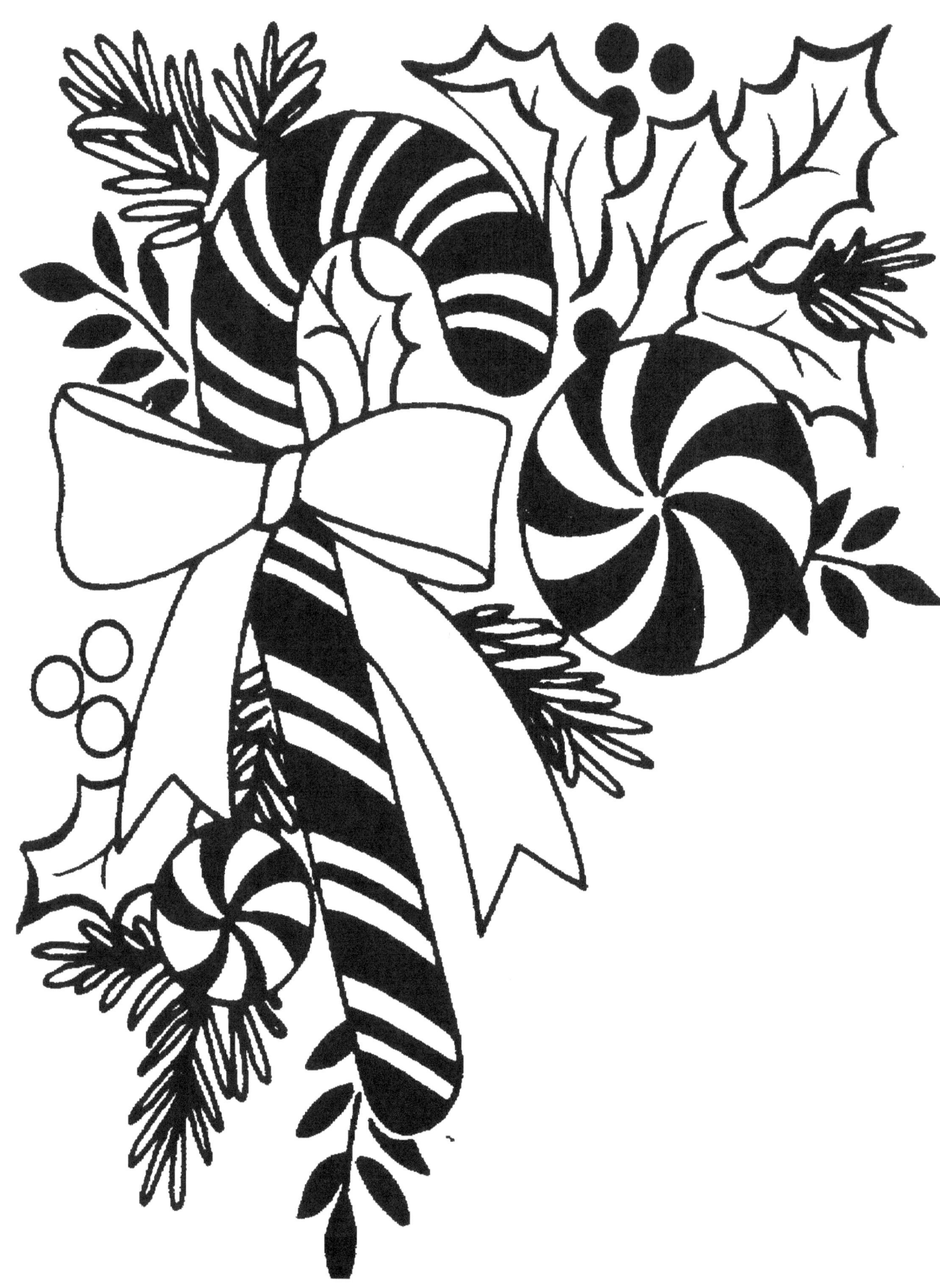

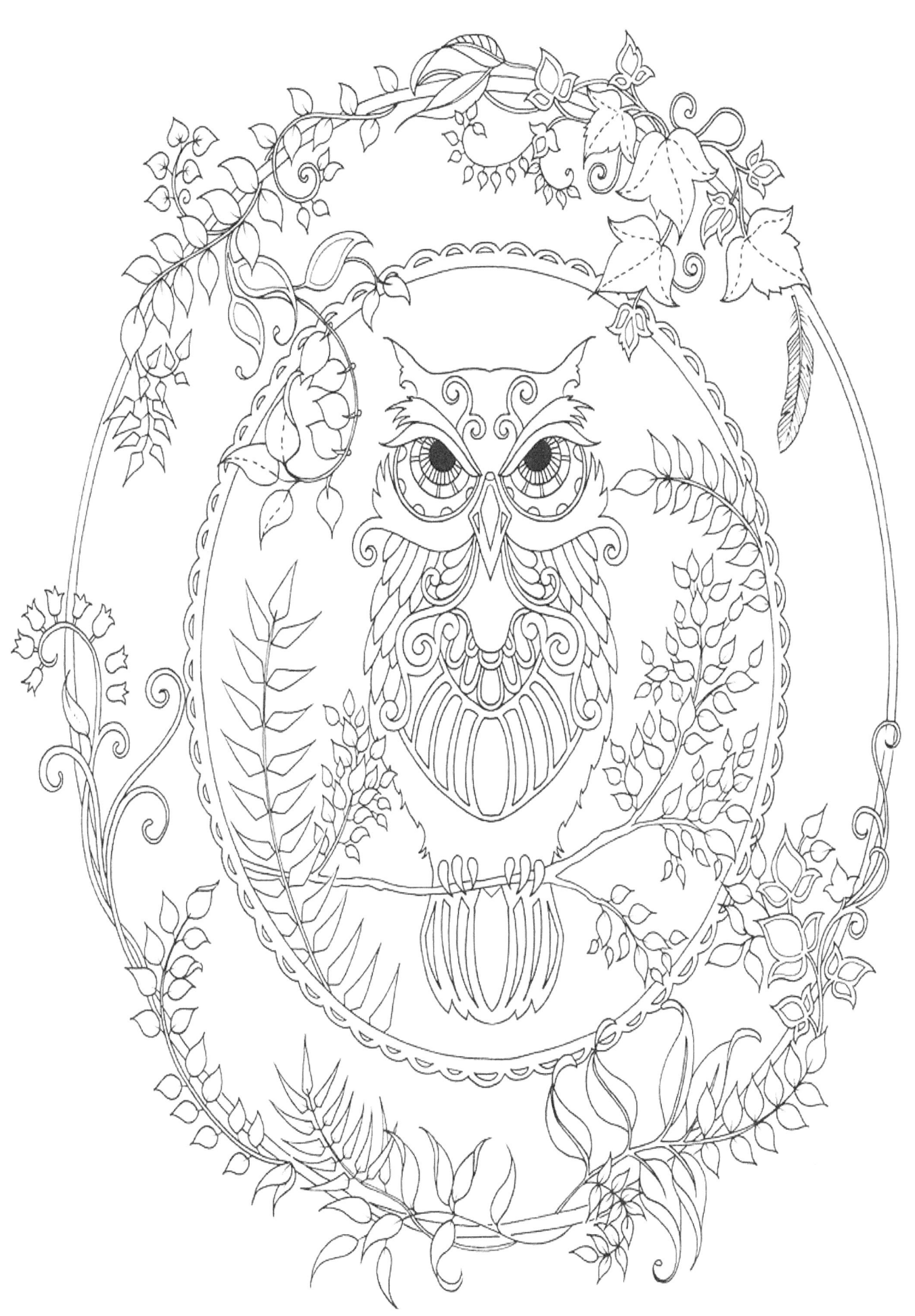

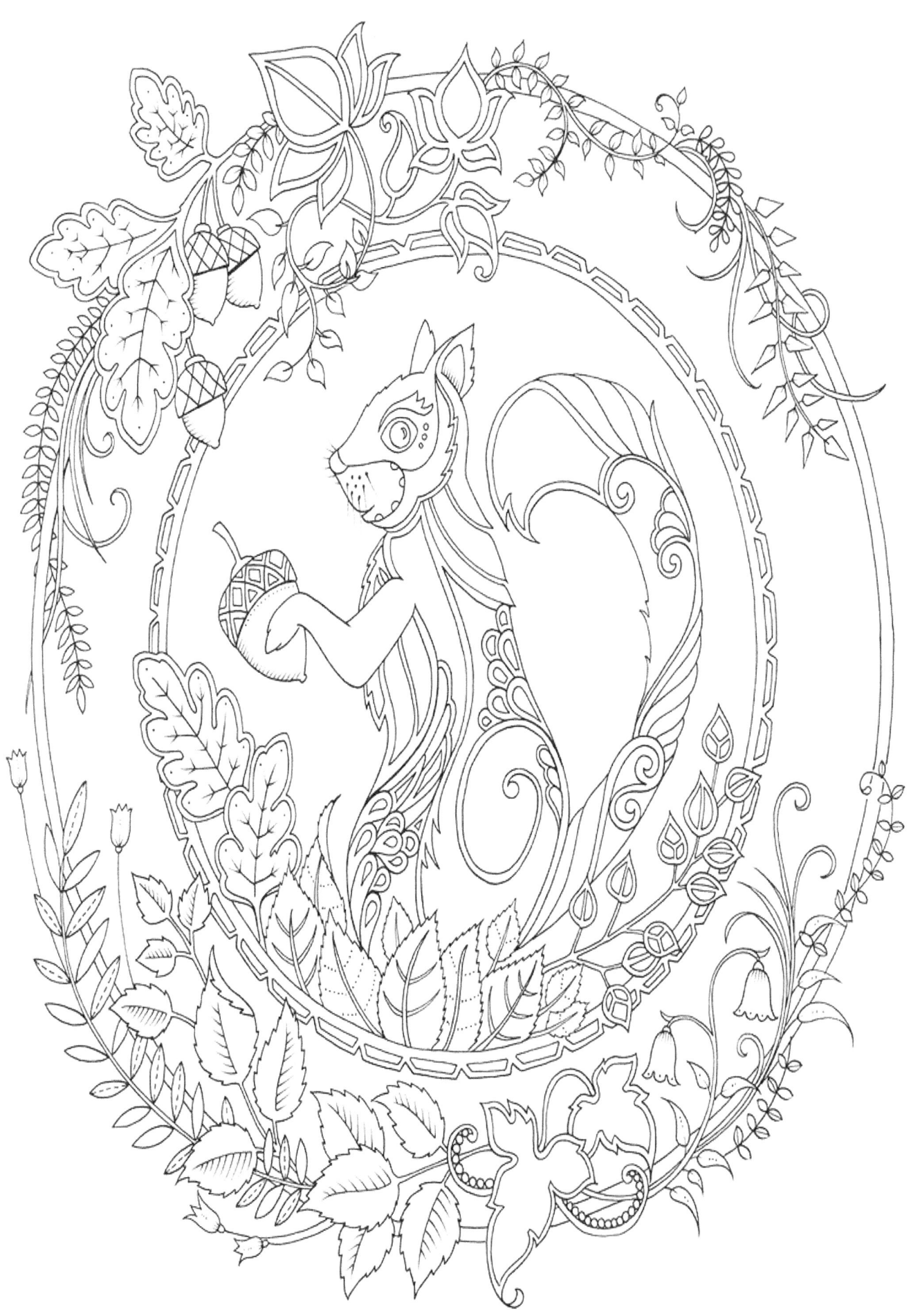

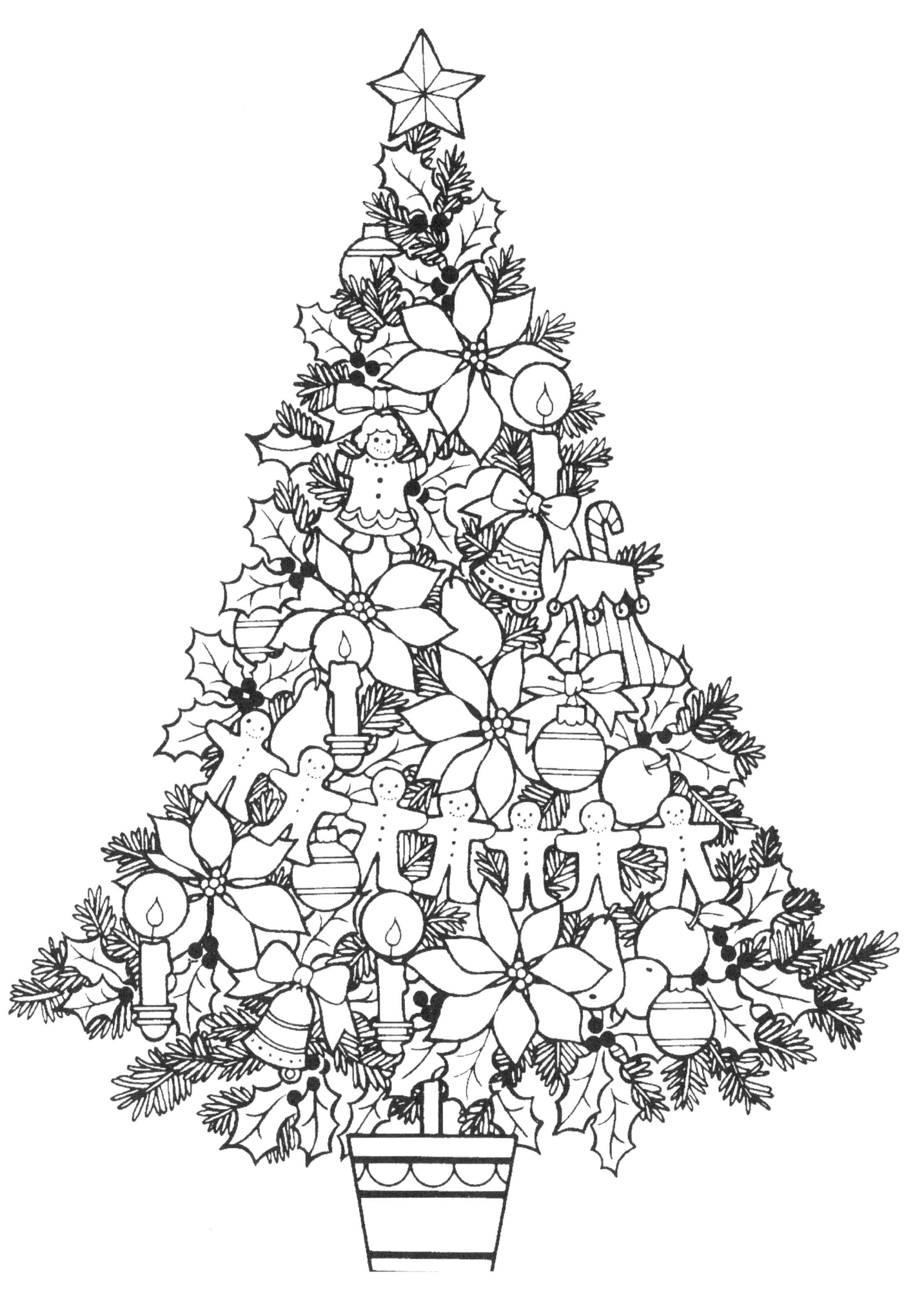

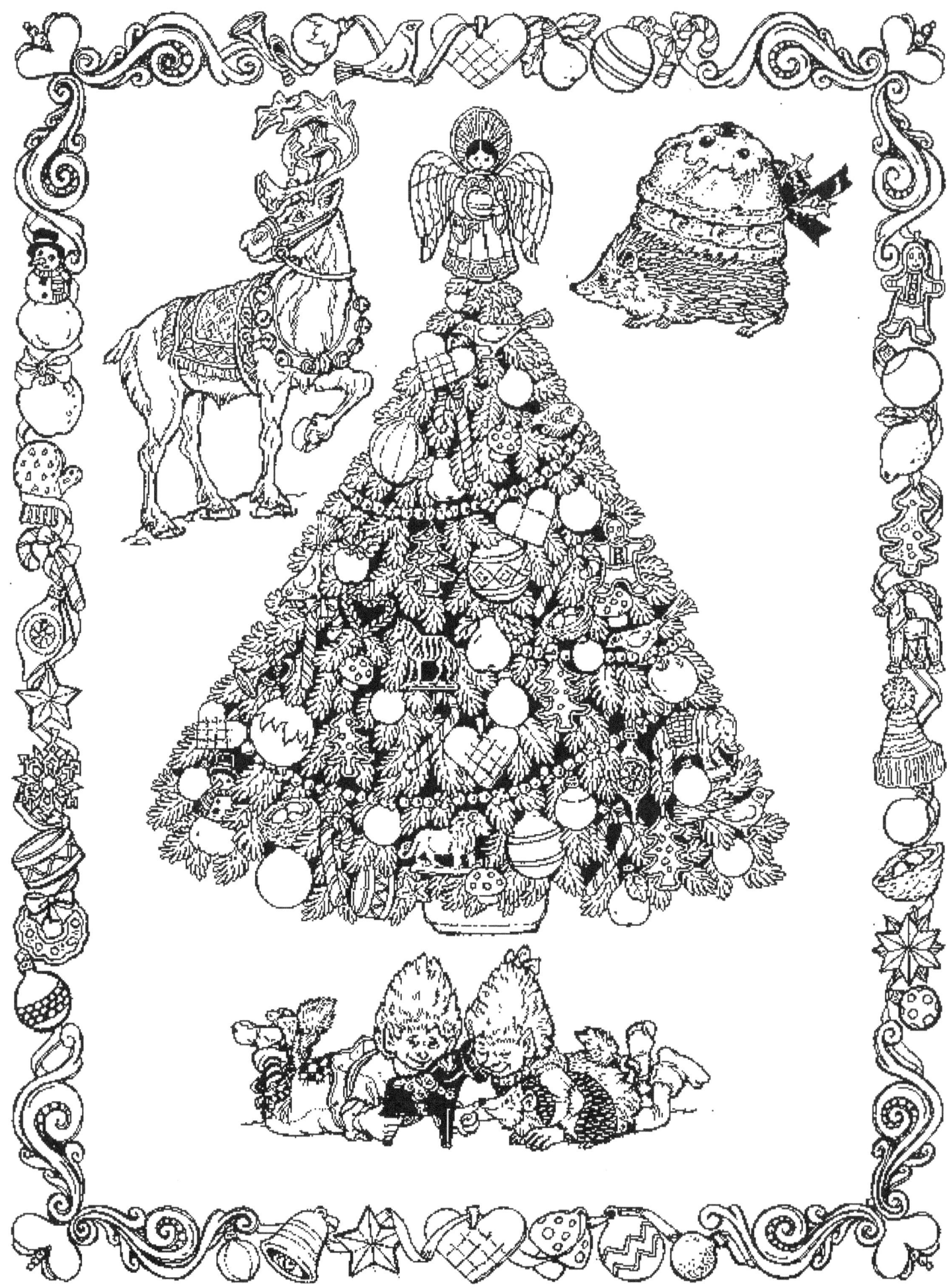

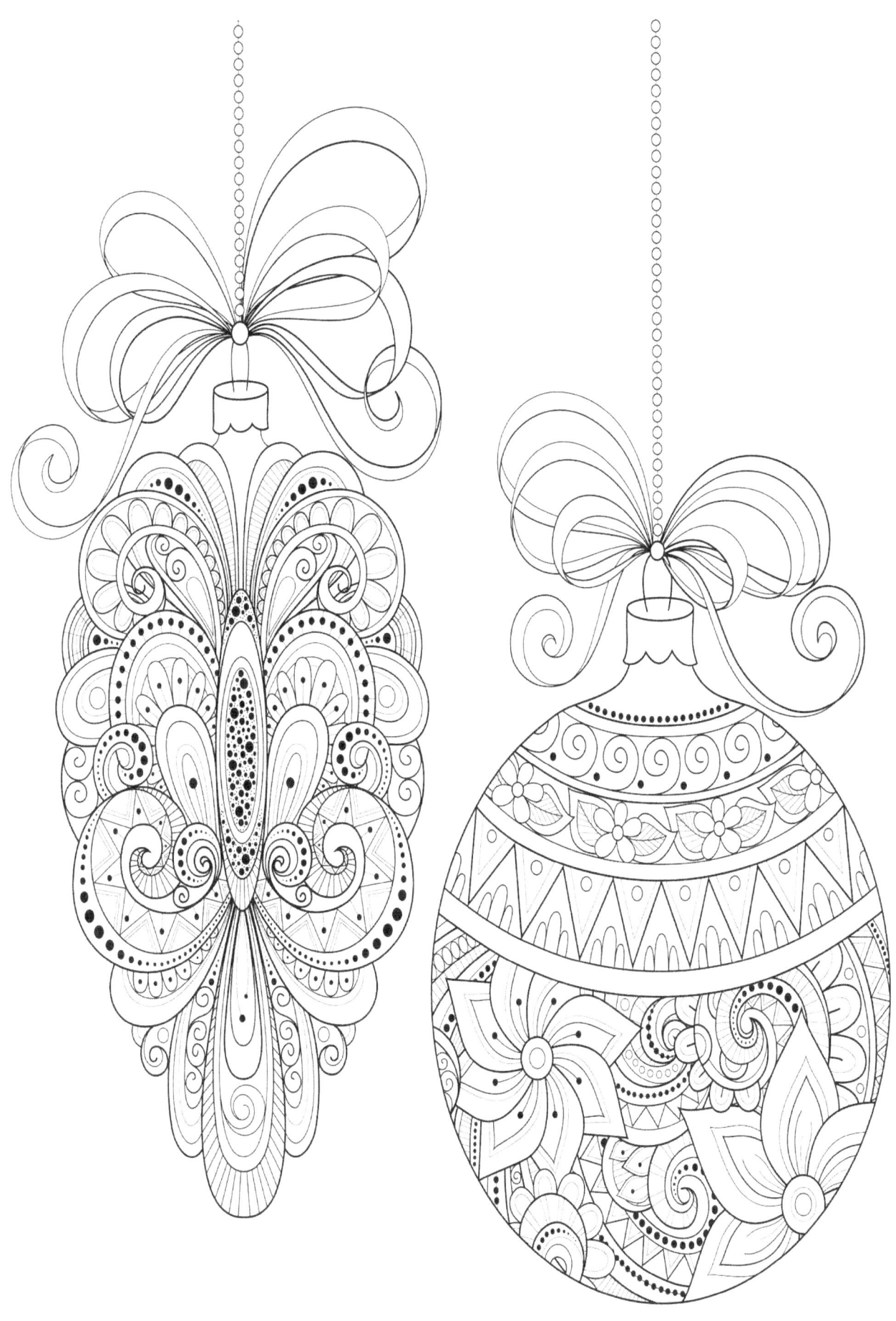

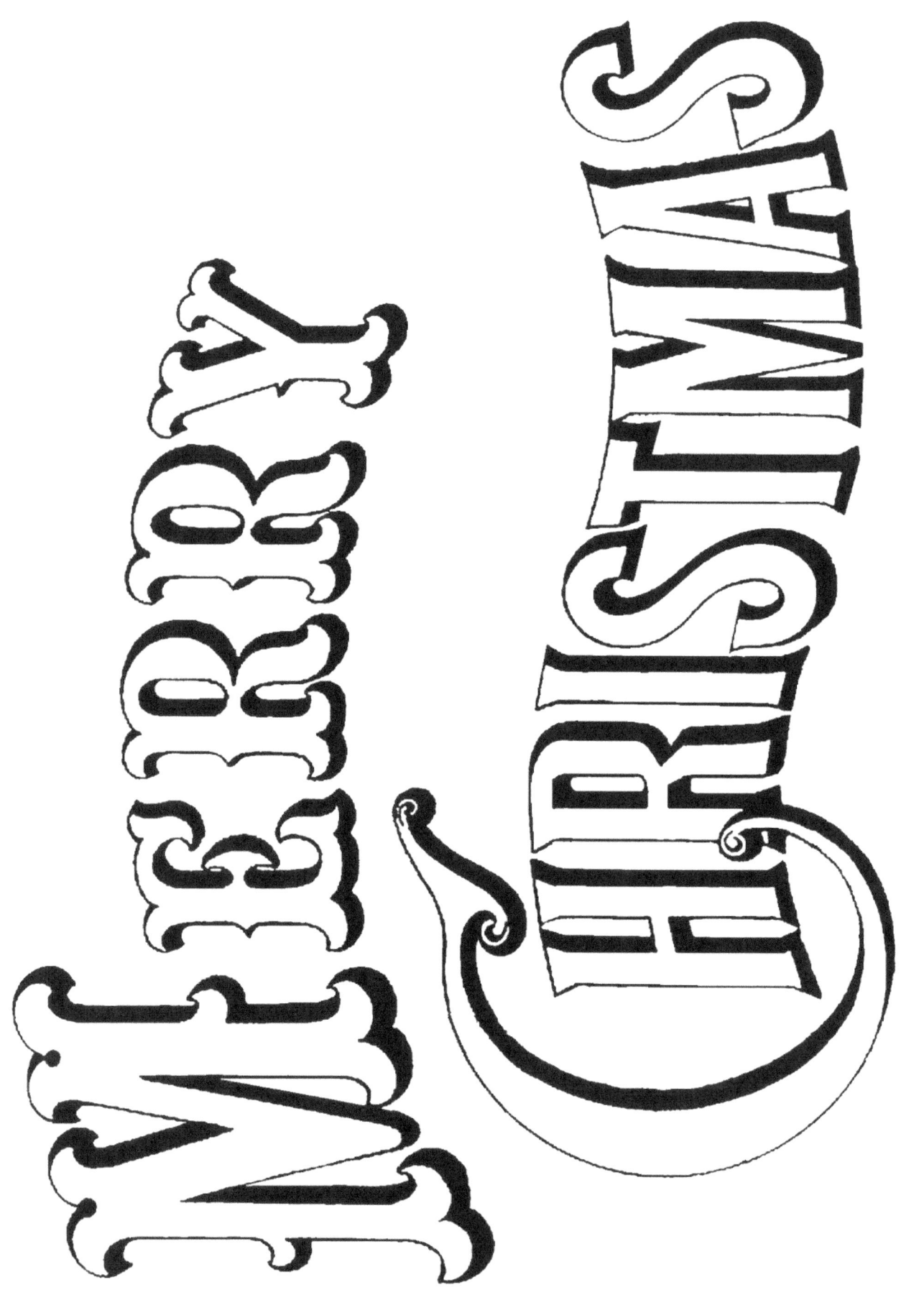

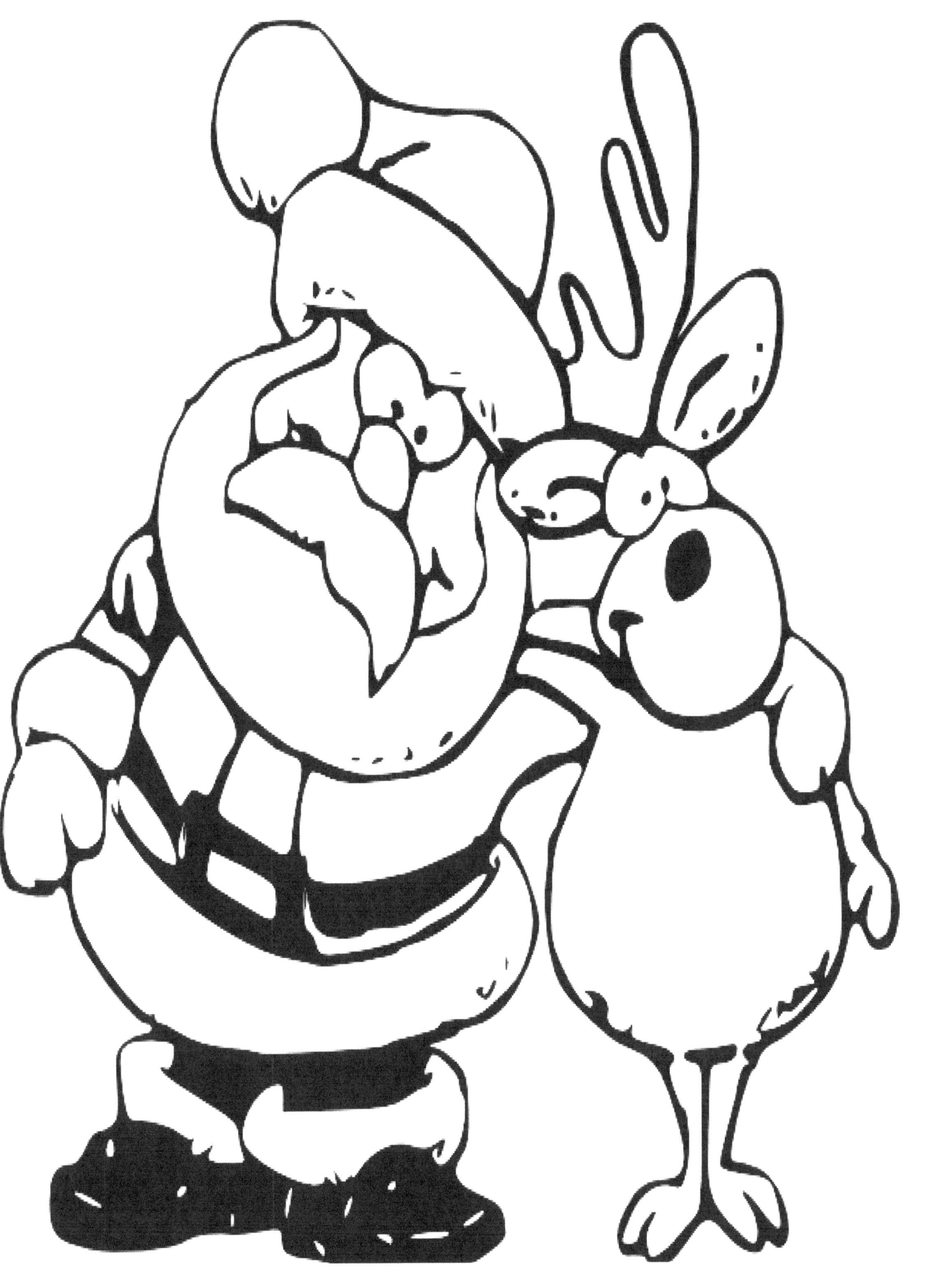

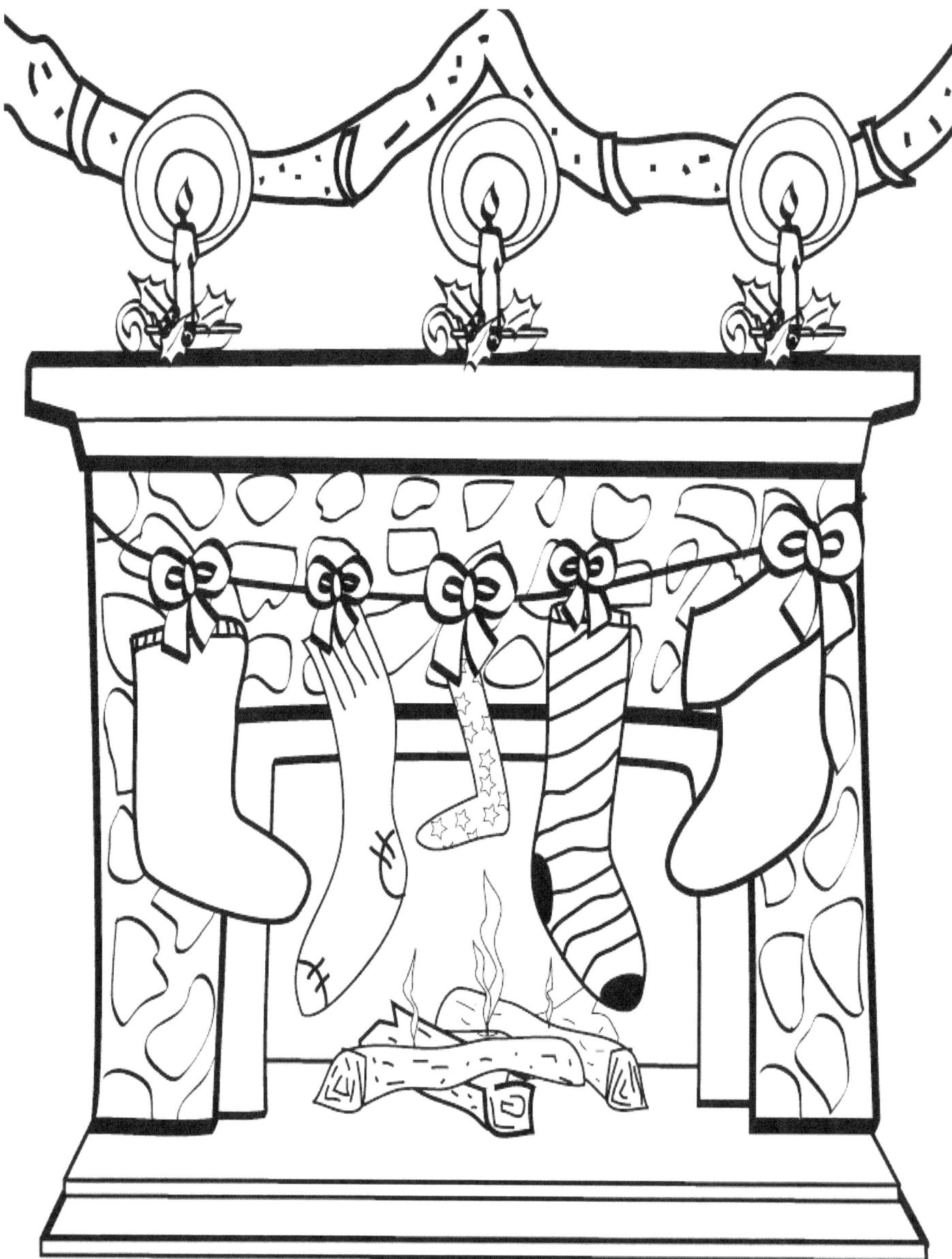

Myrtille

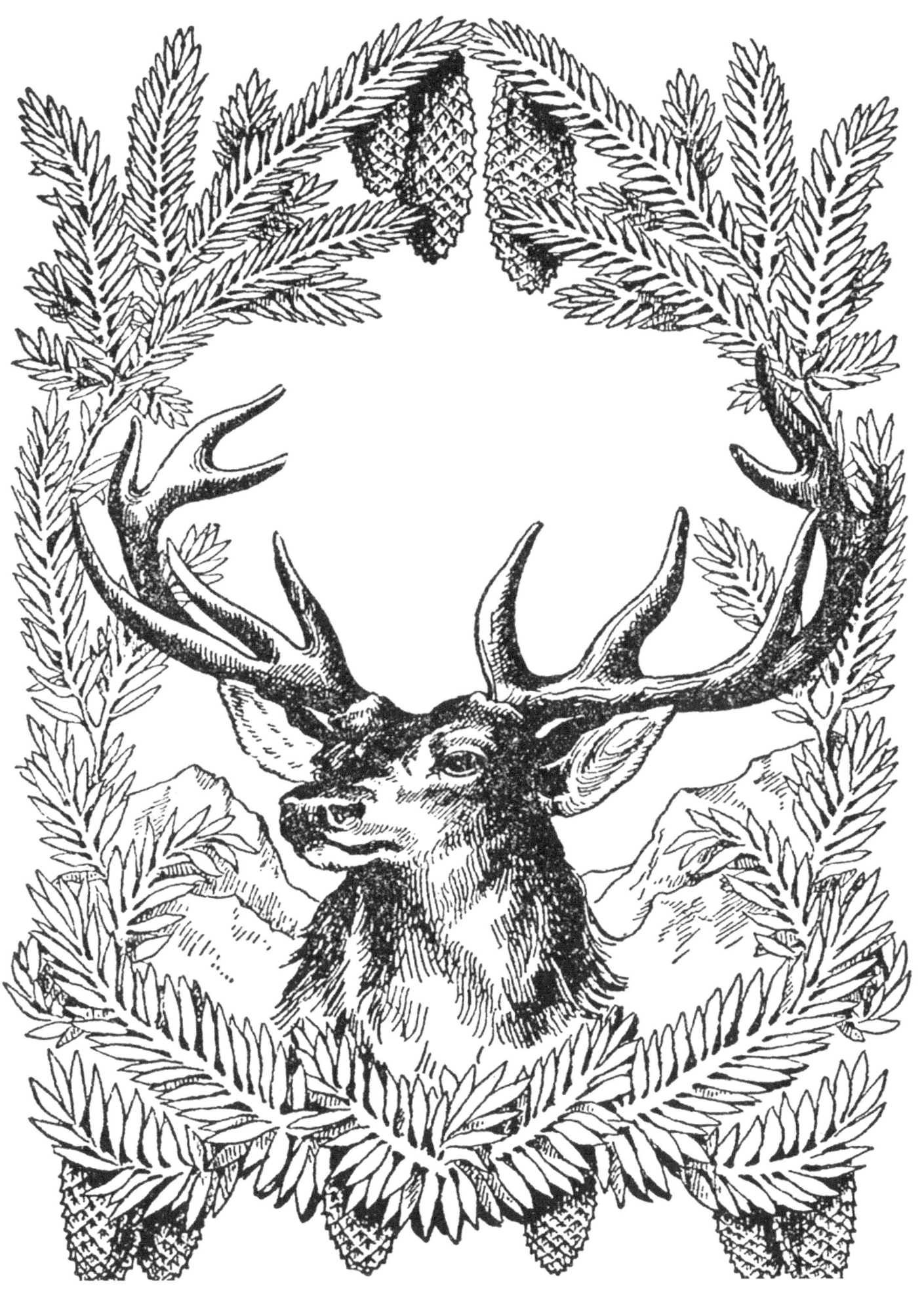

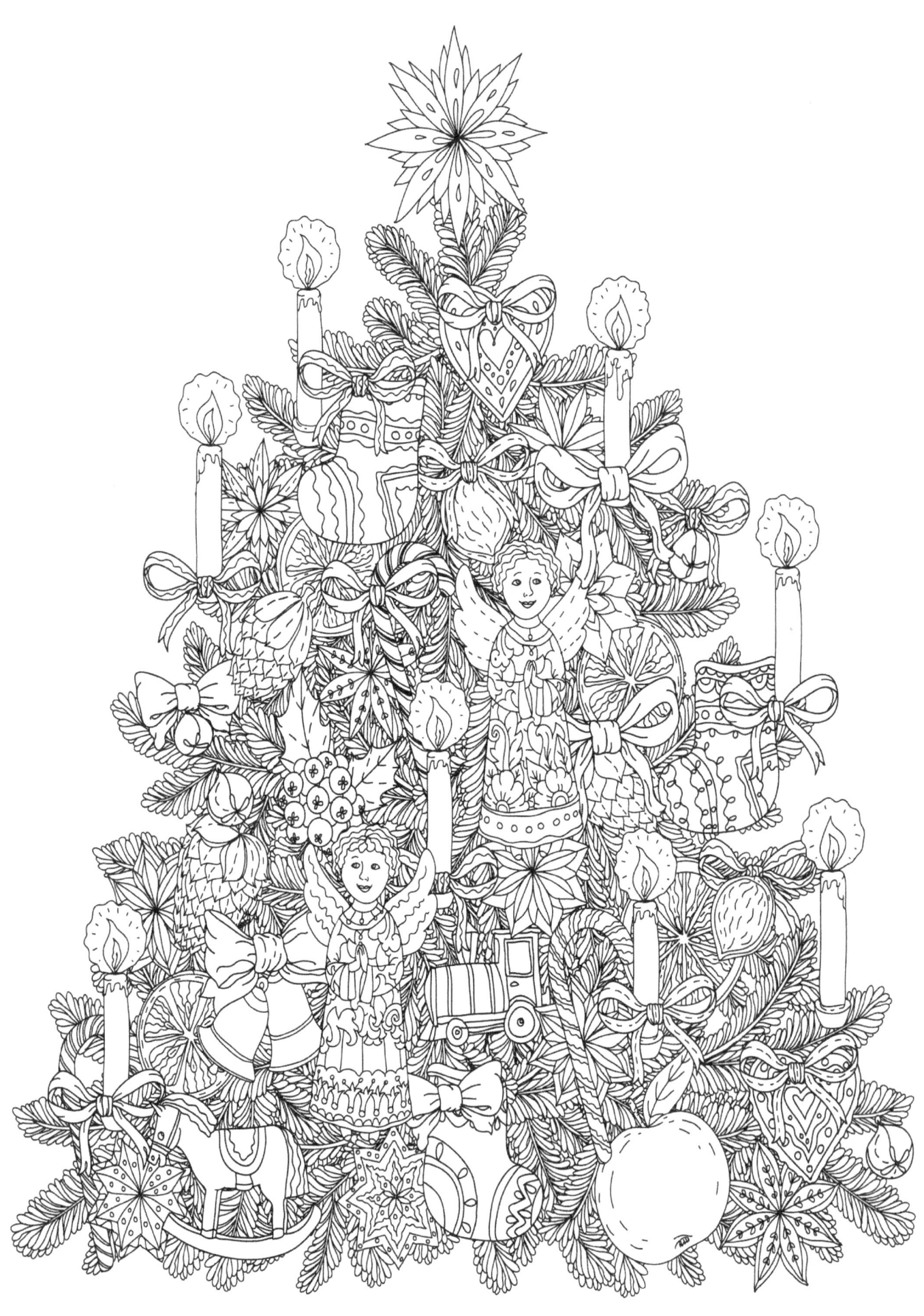

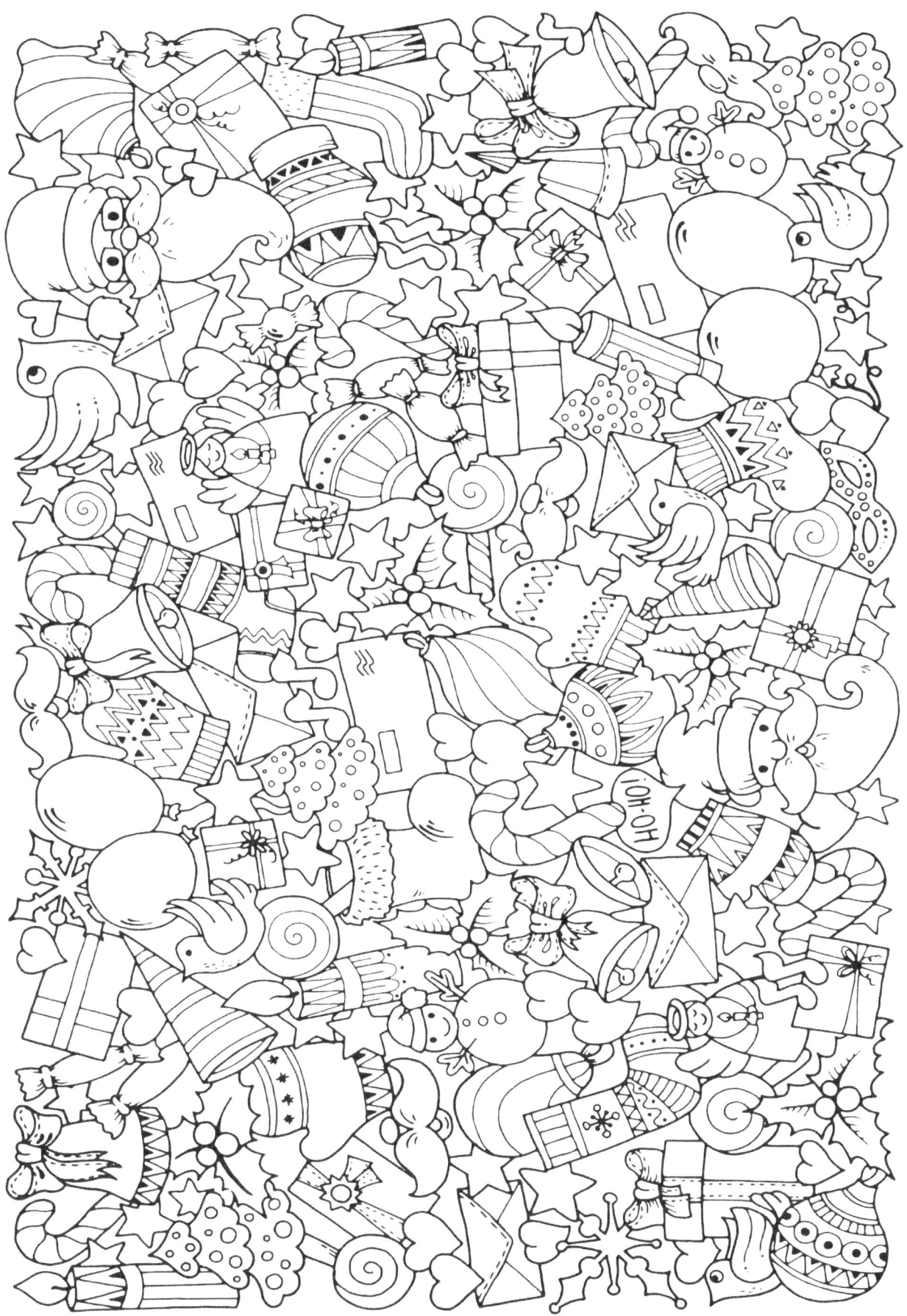

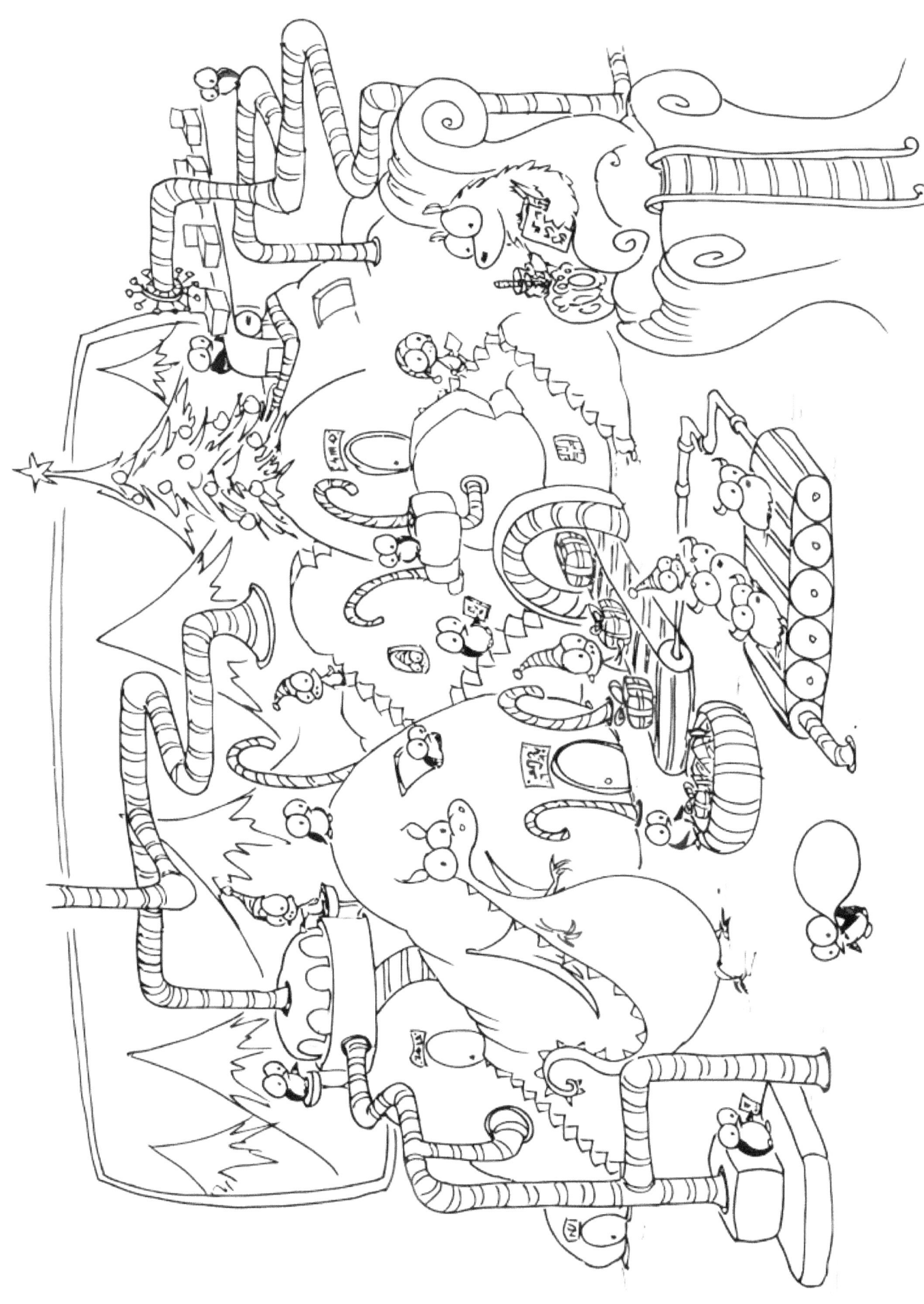

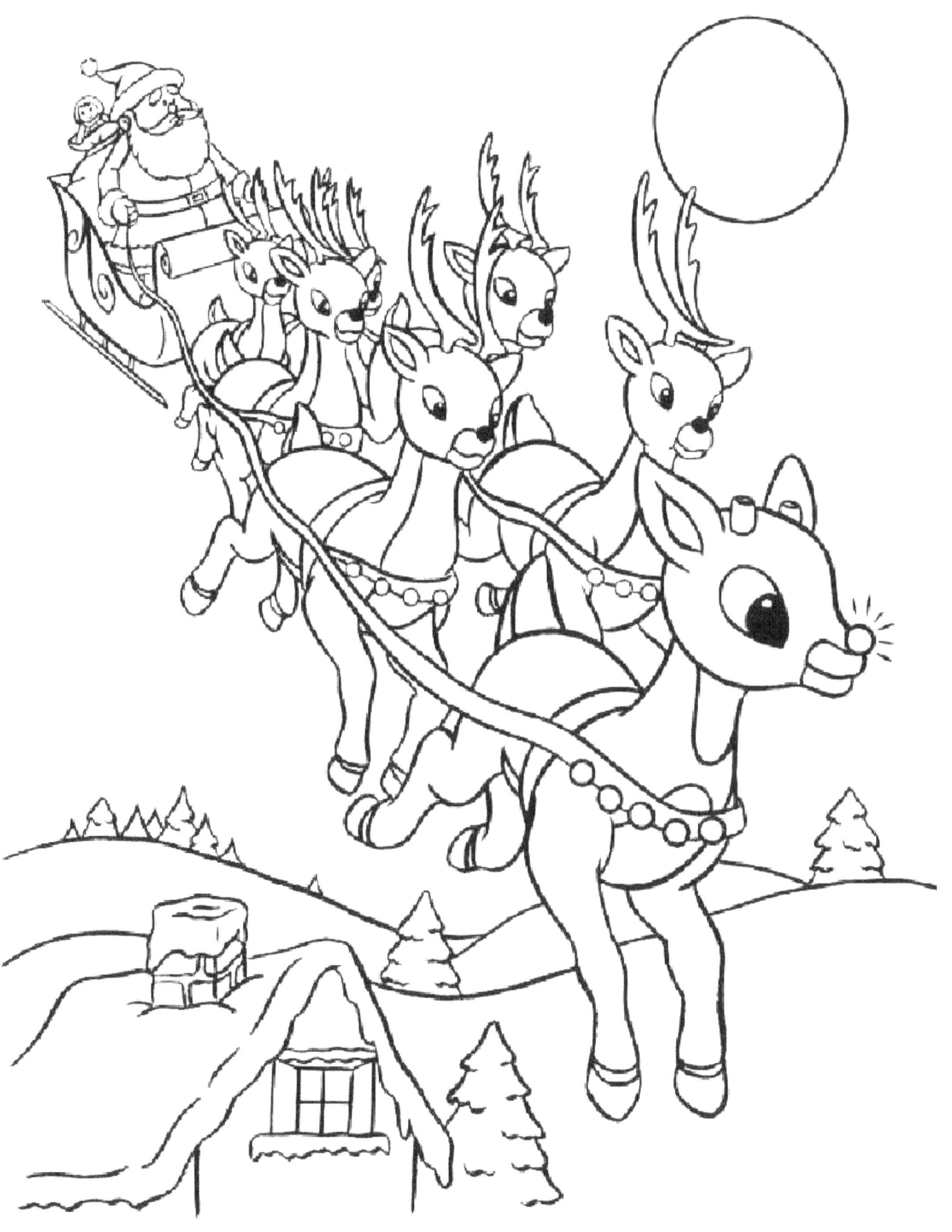

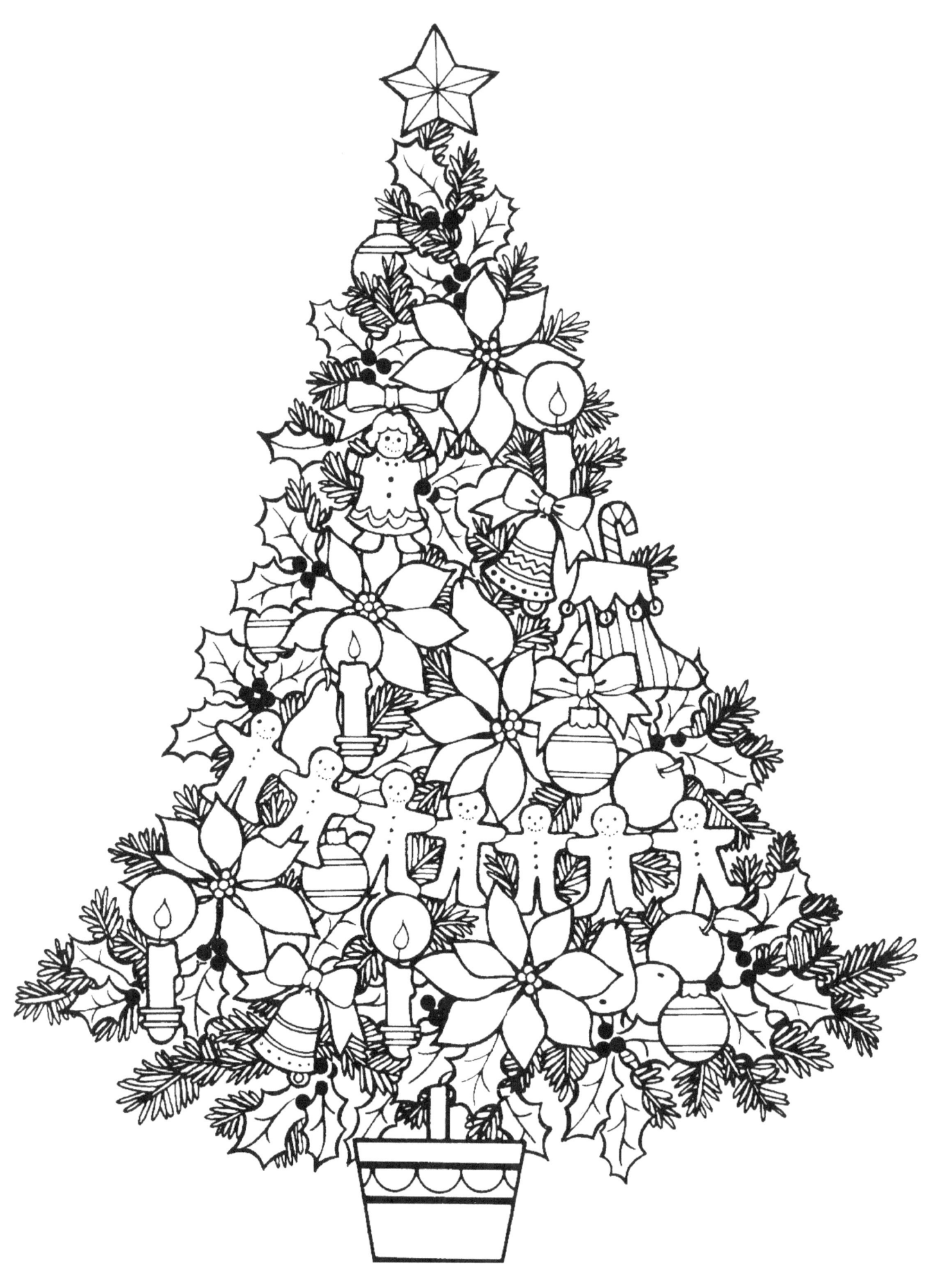

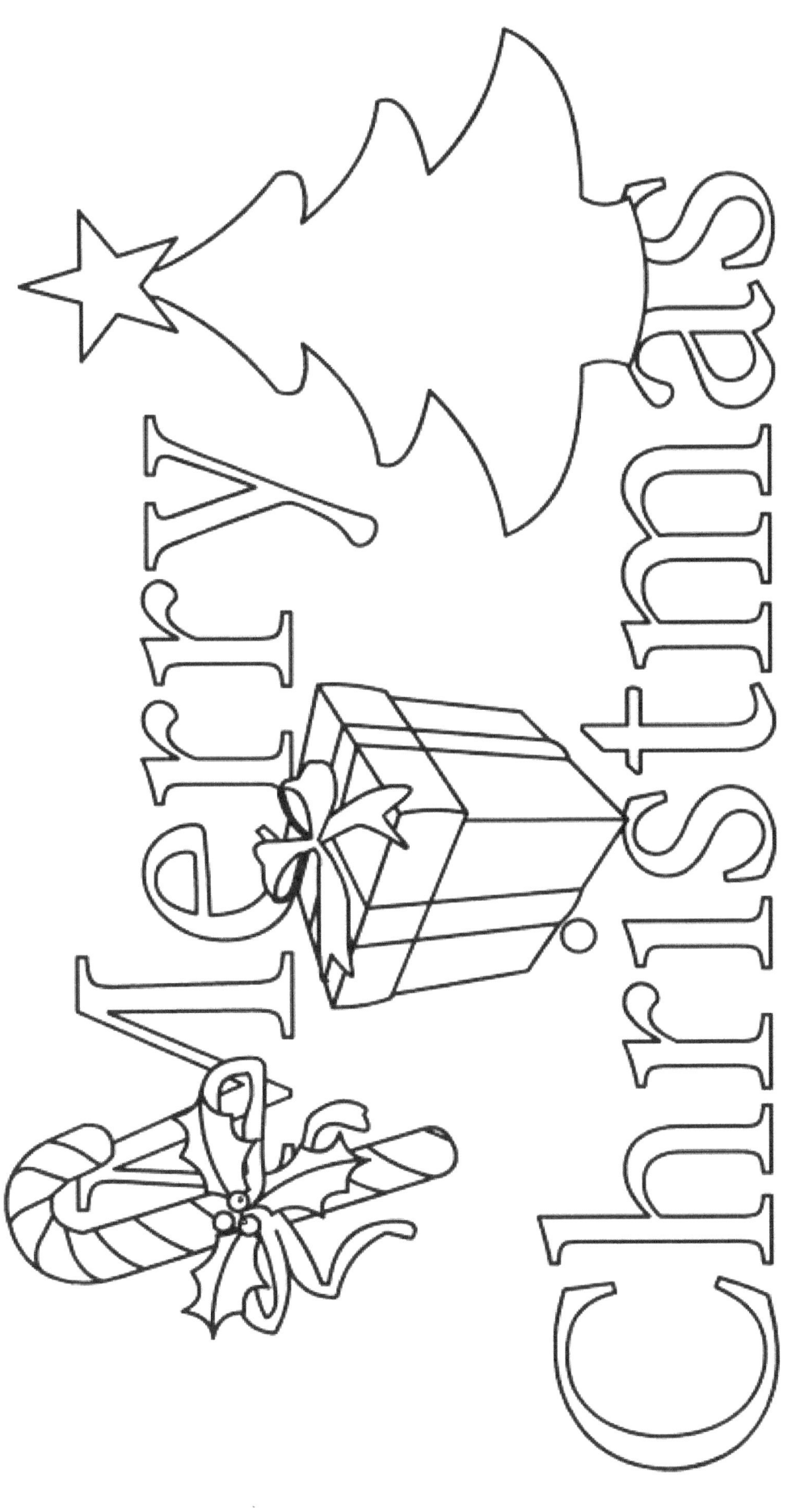

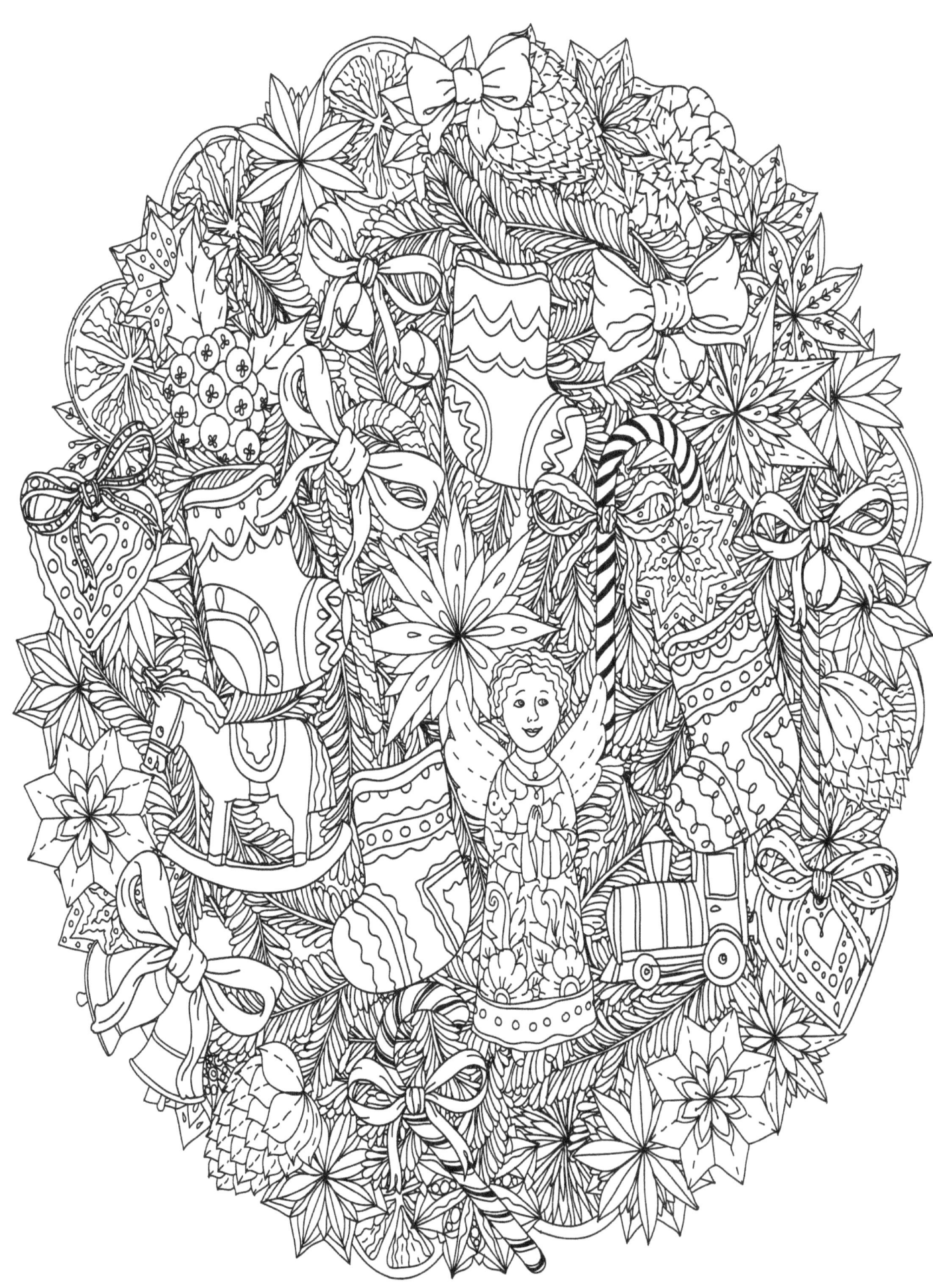

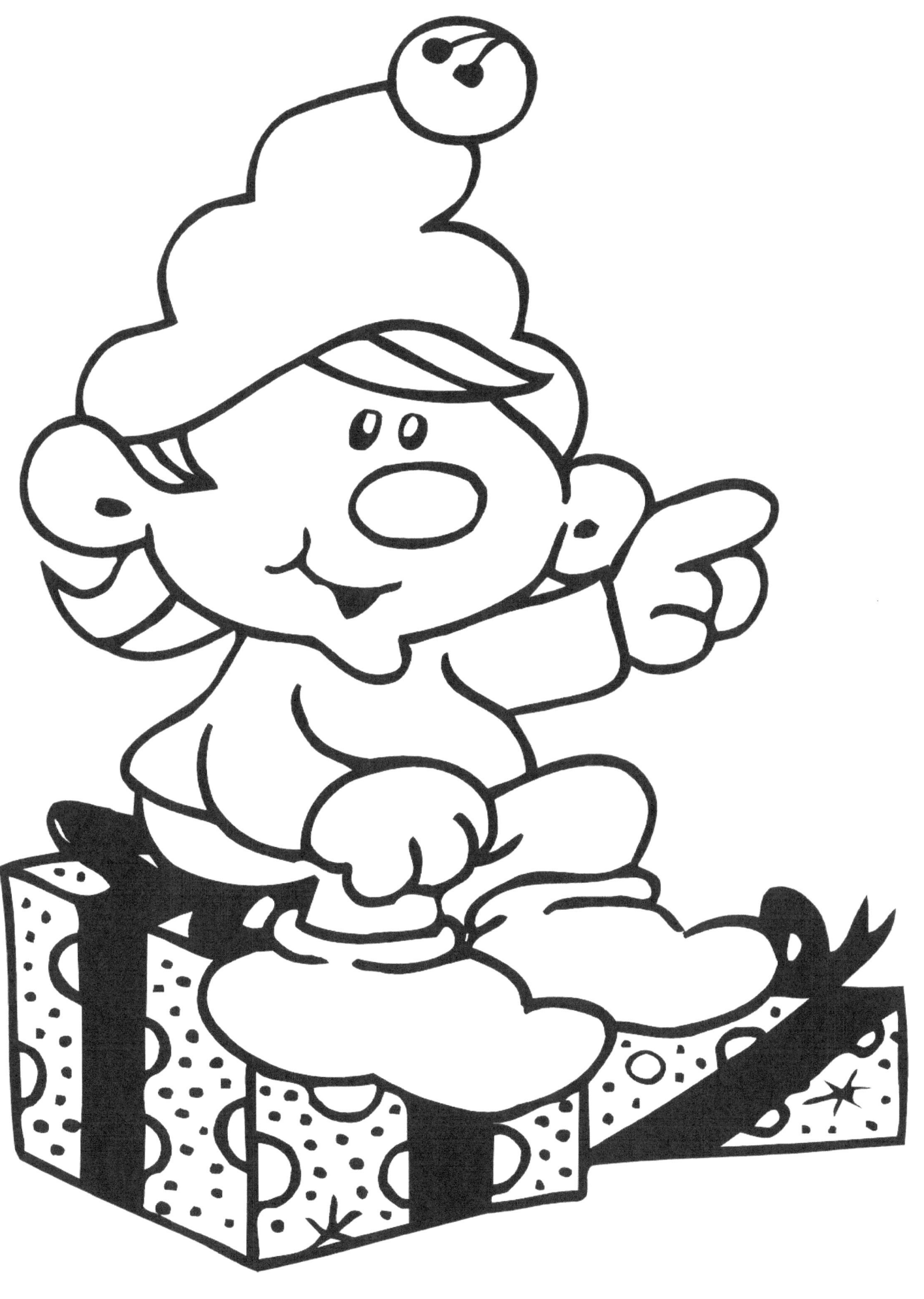

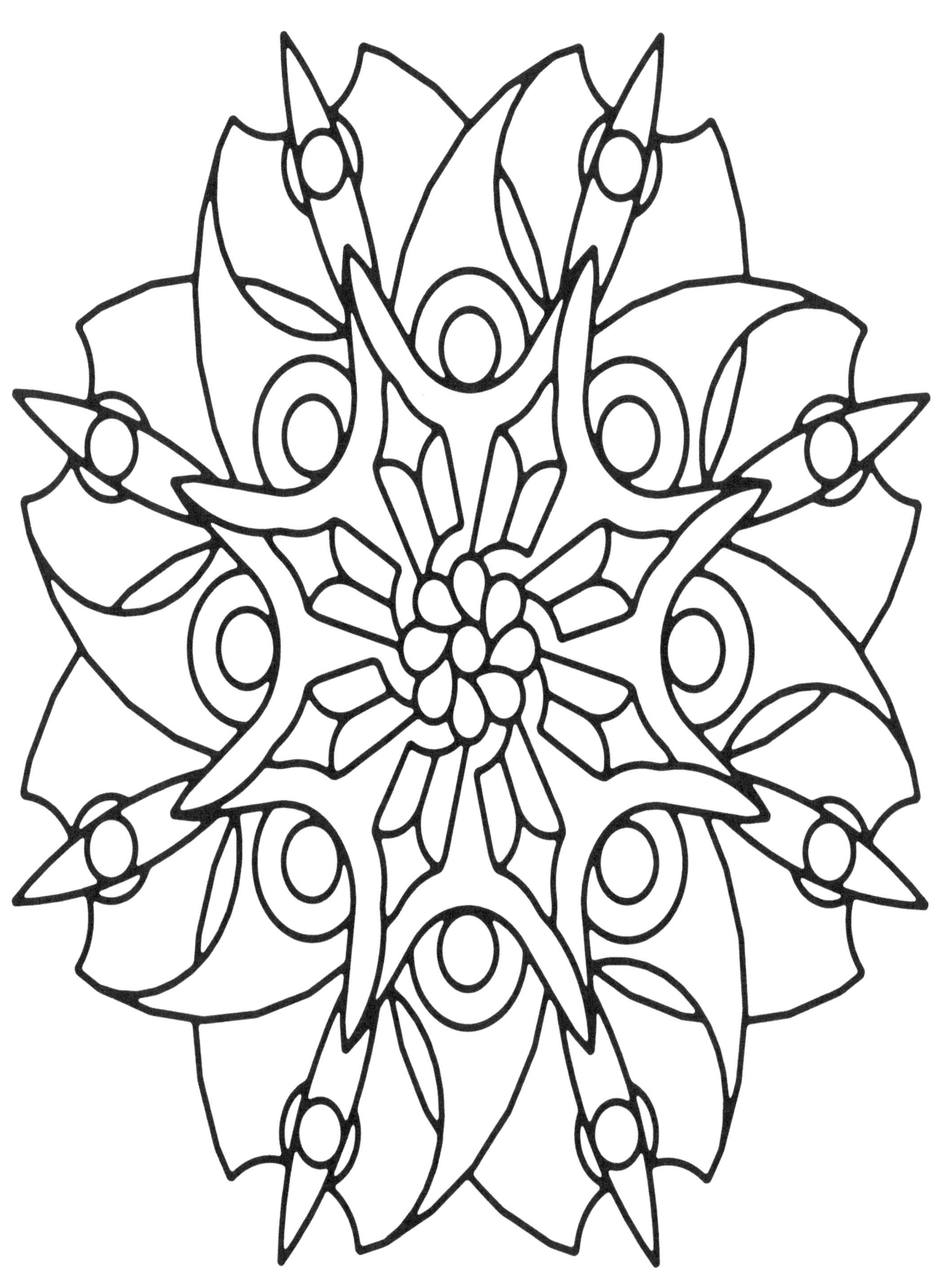

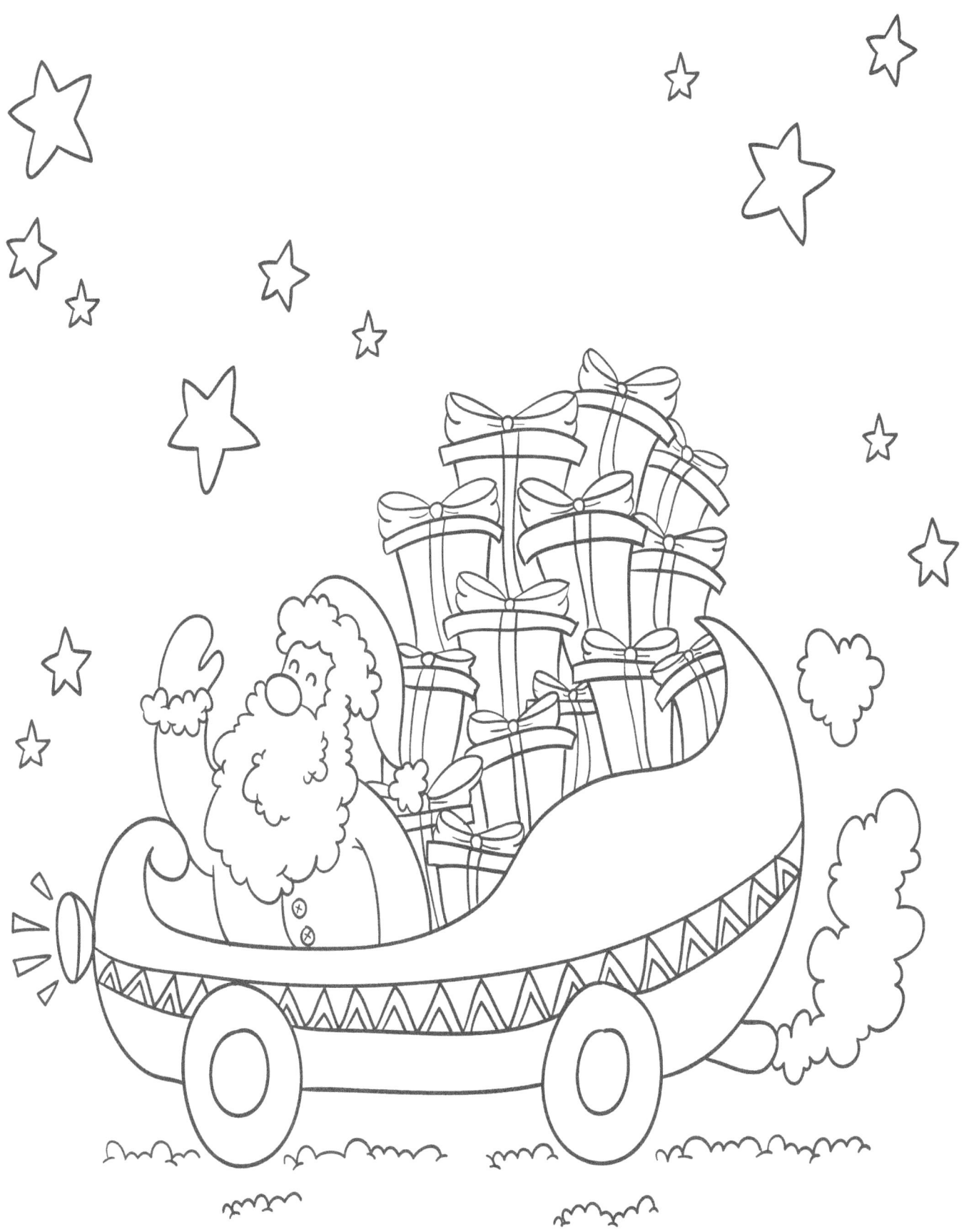

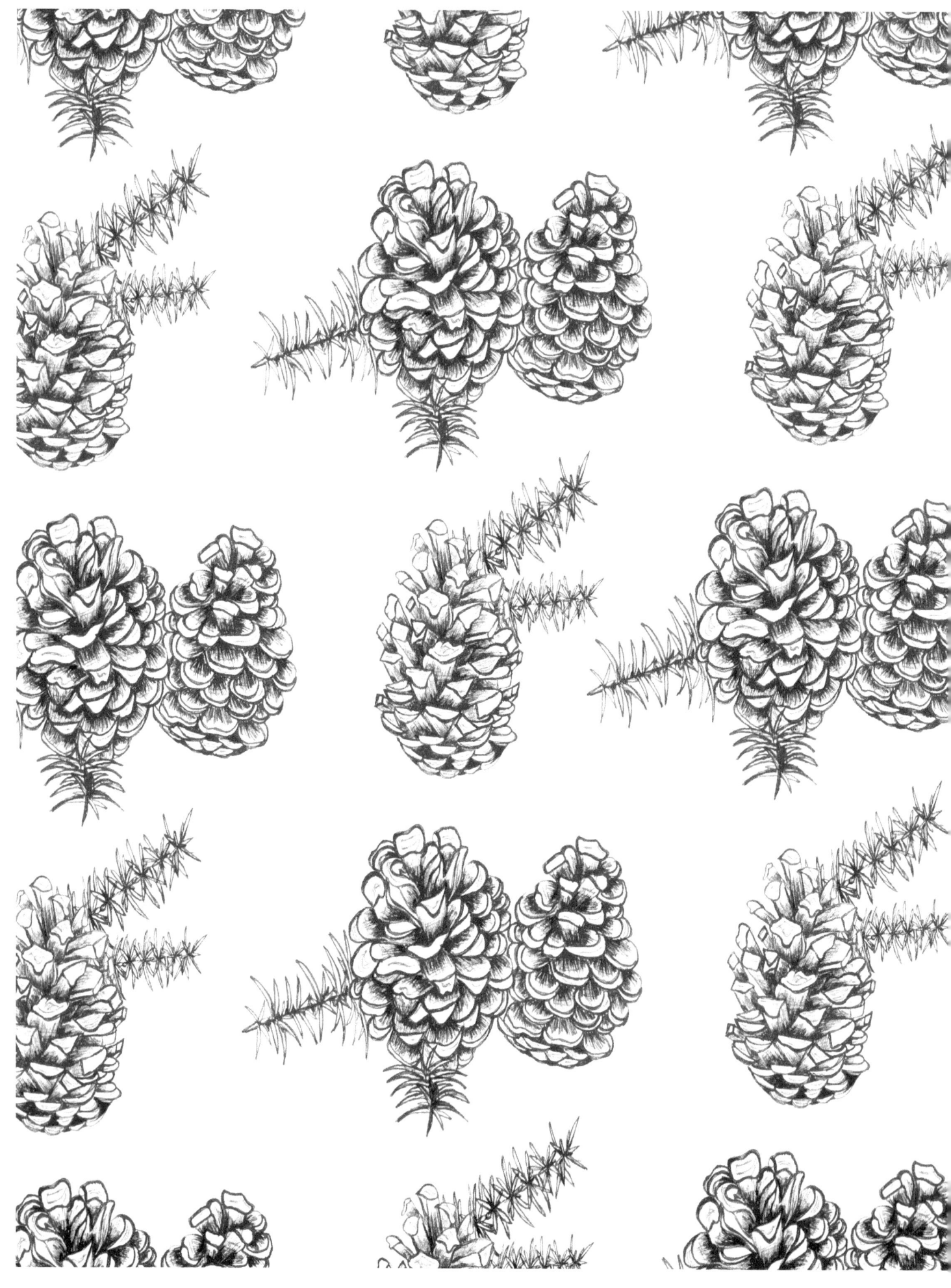

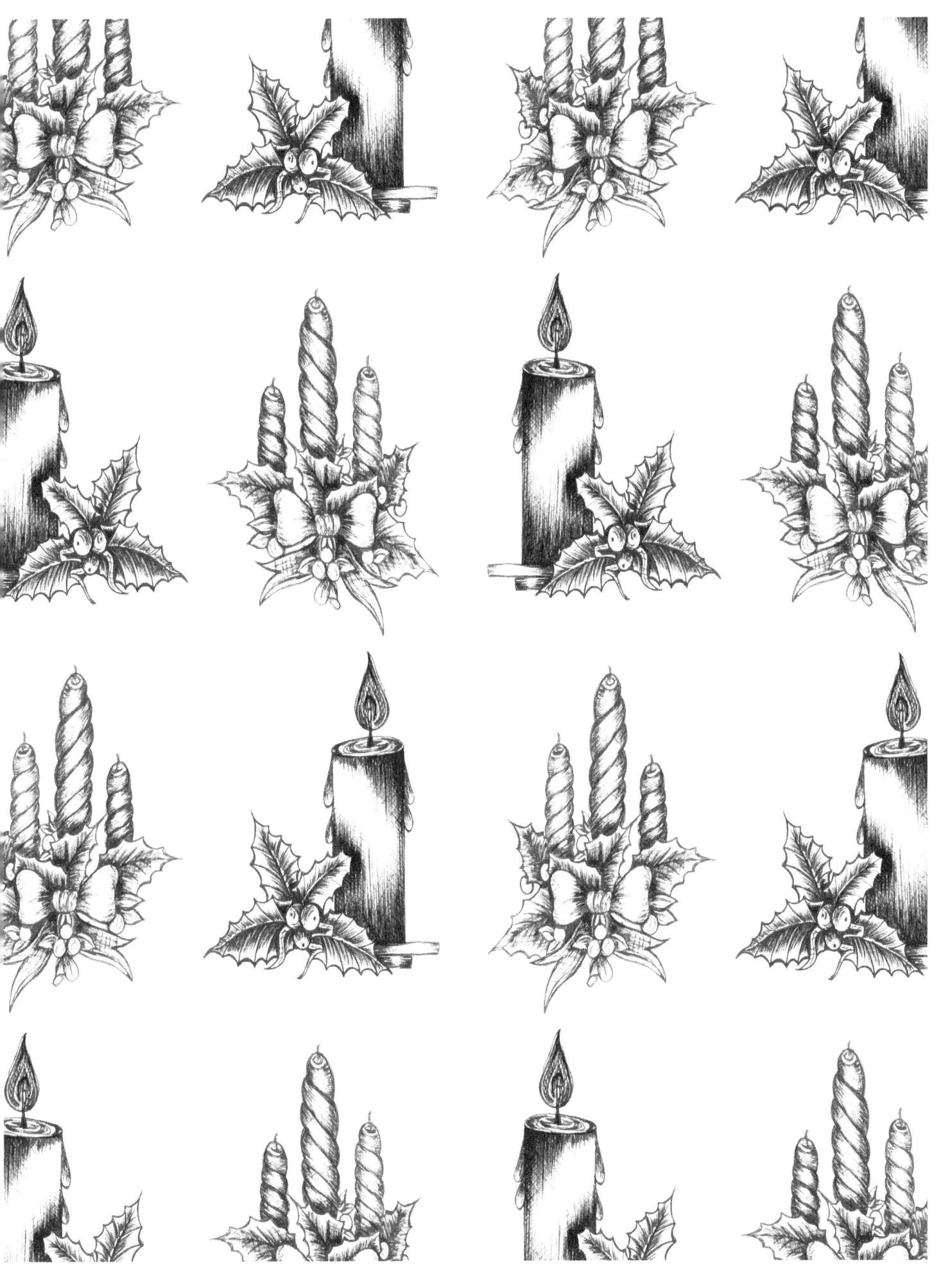

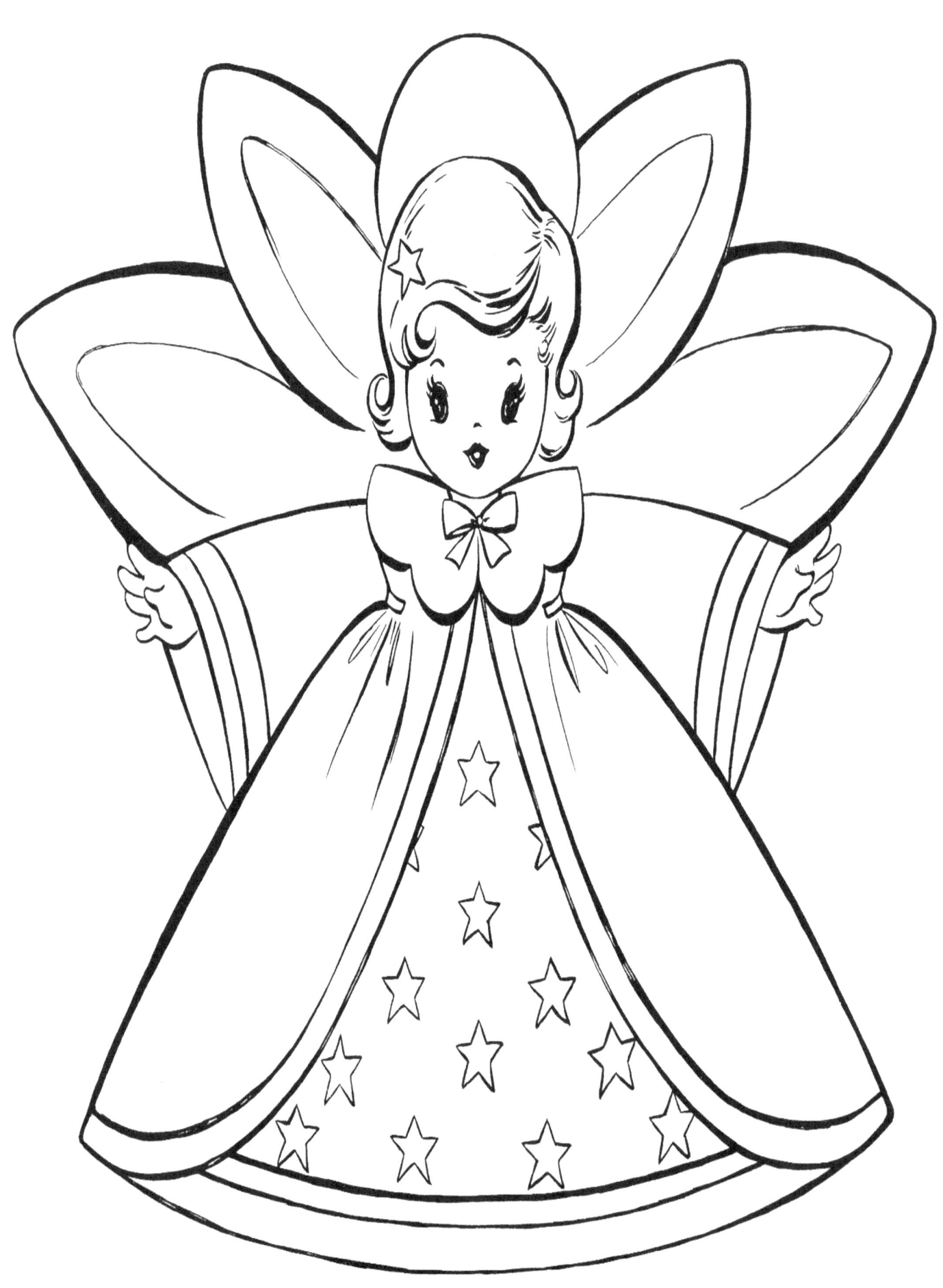

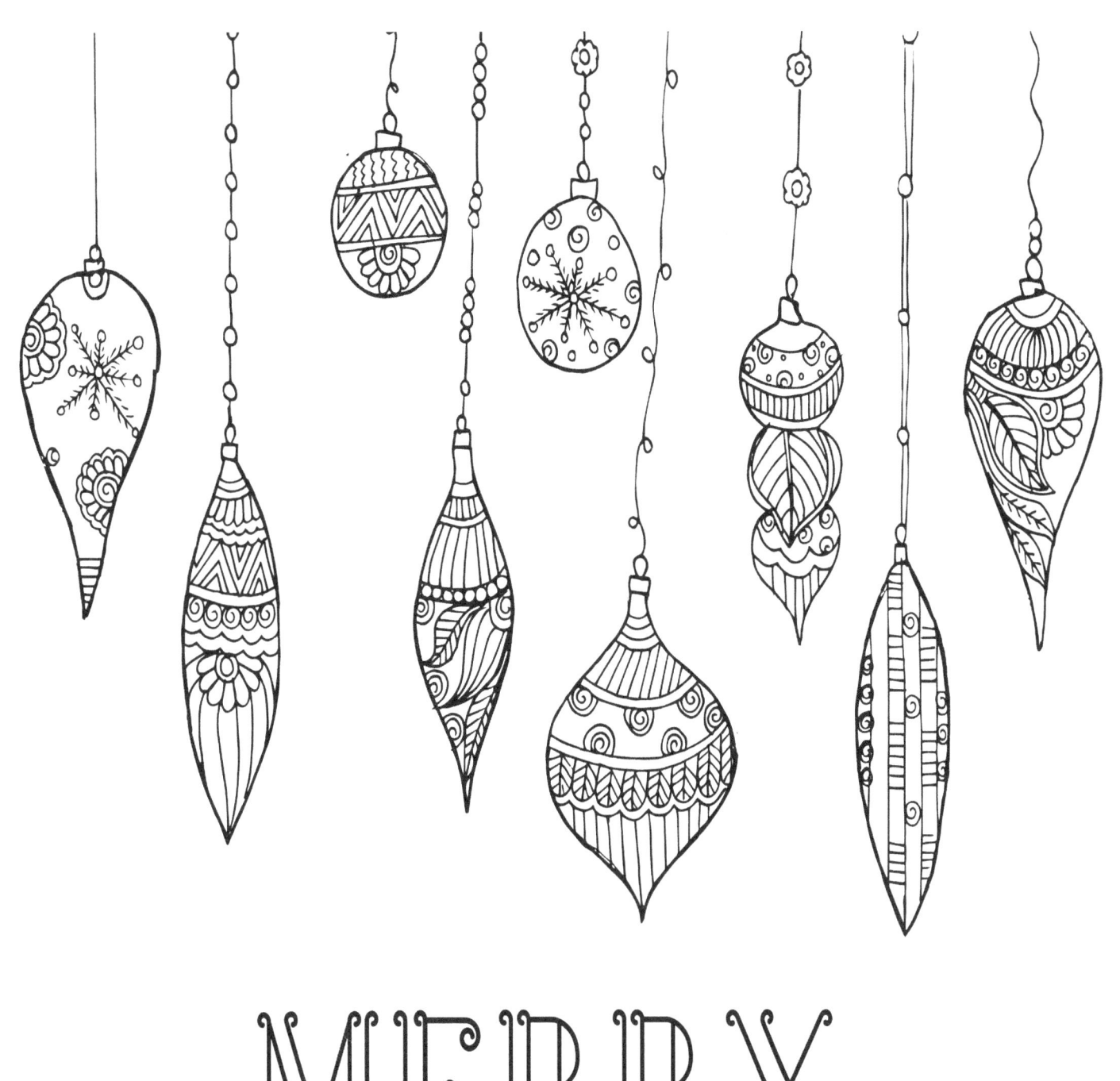

MERRY
CHRISTMAS

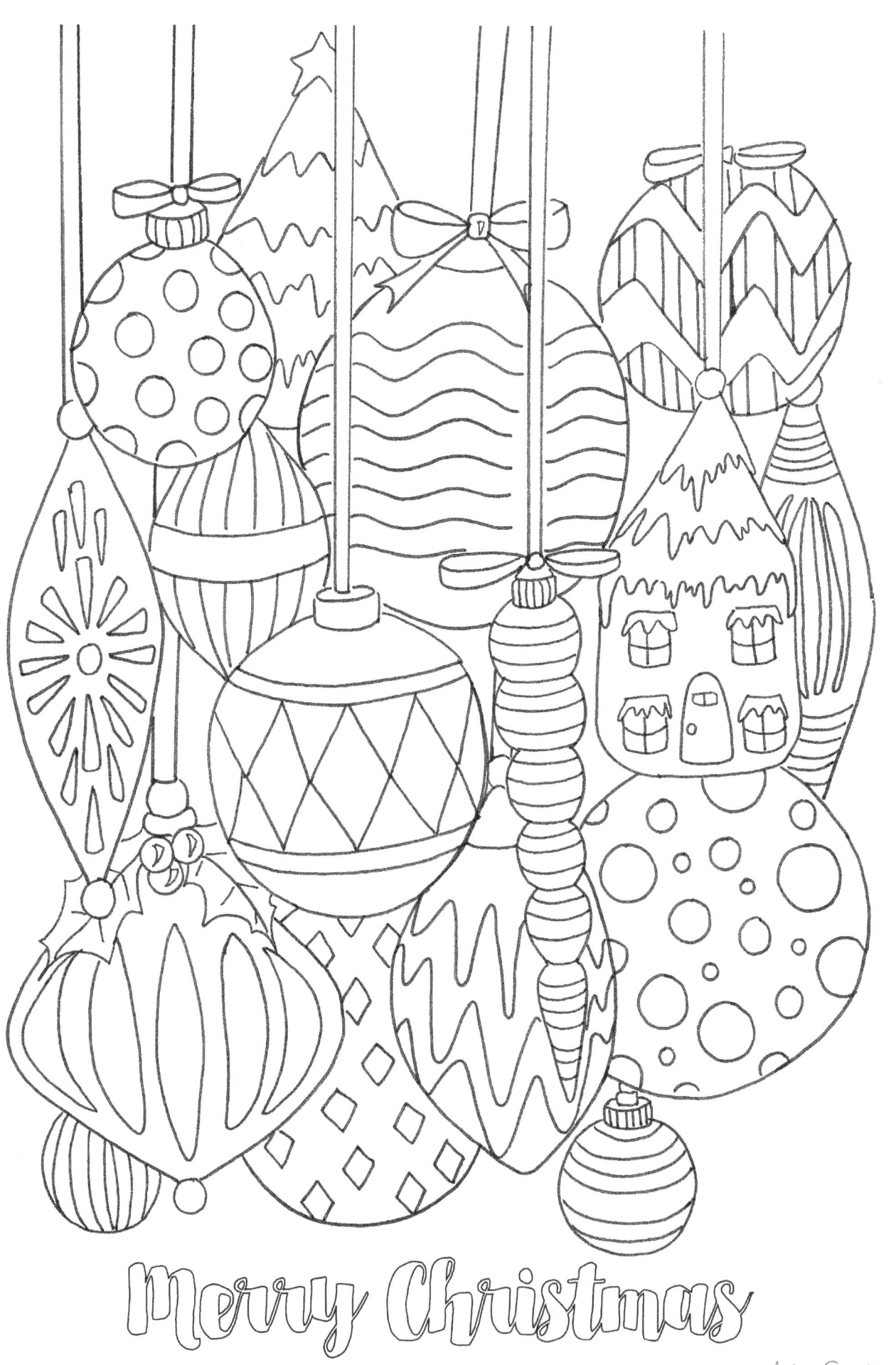

Merry Christmas

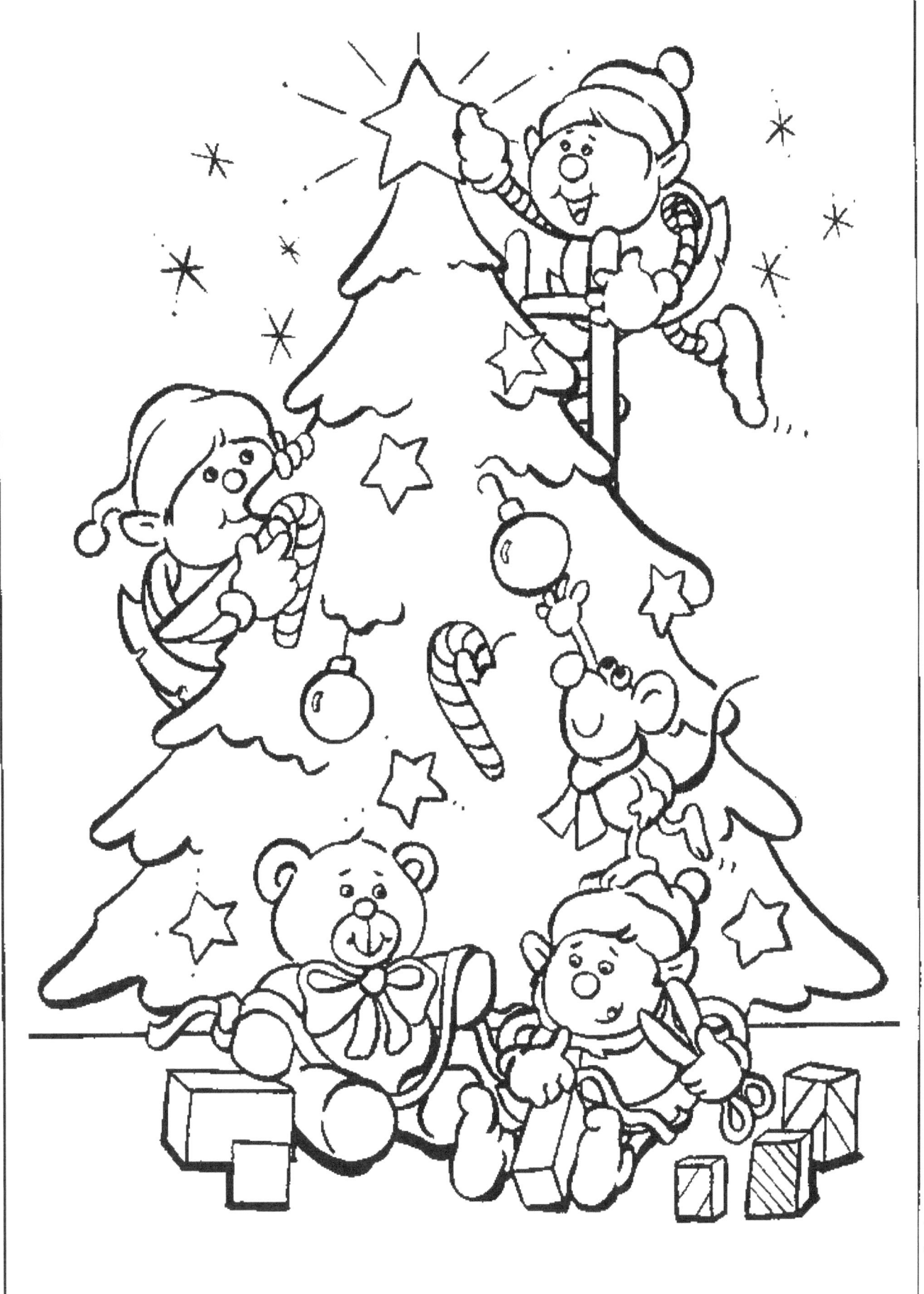

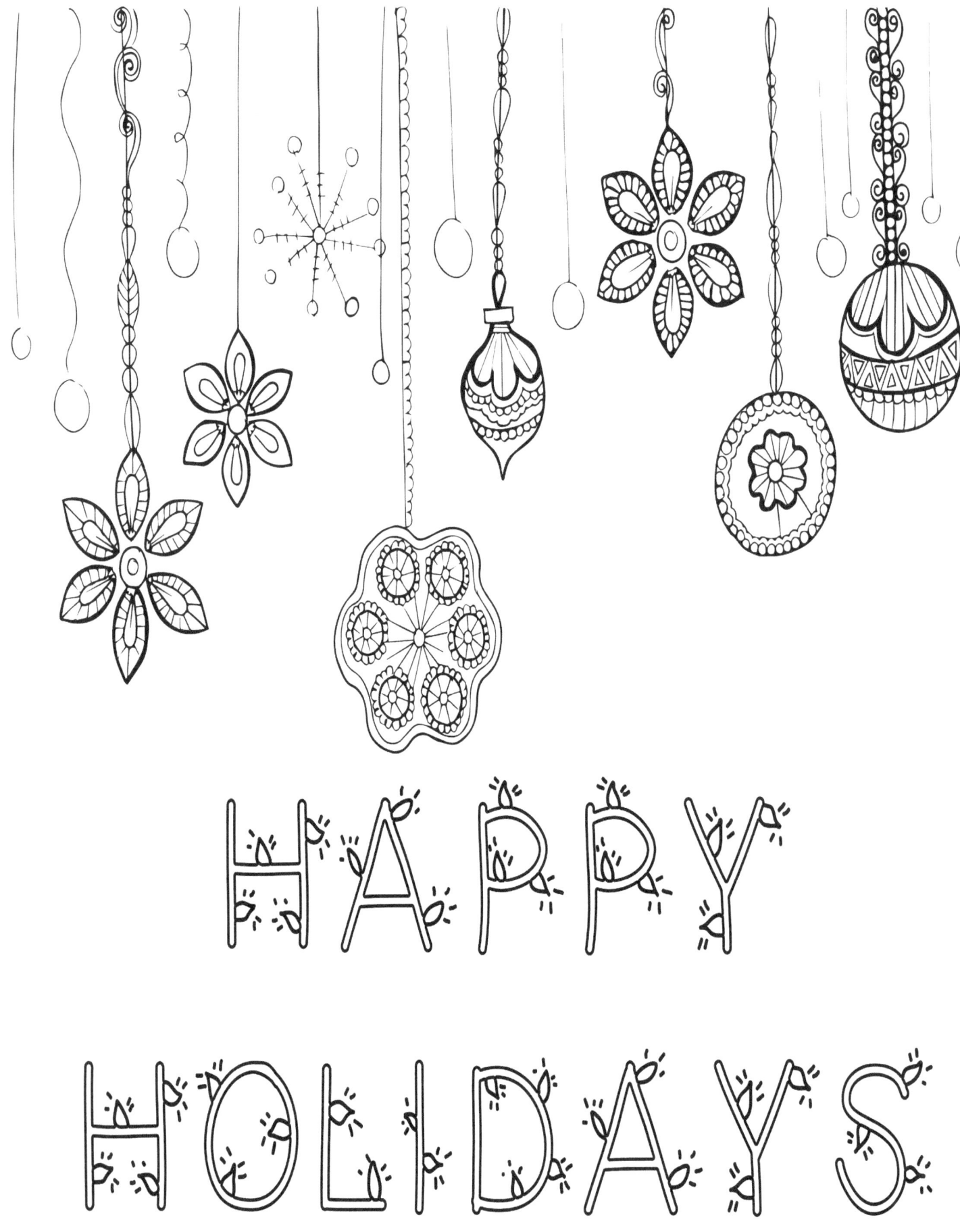

CHRISTMAS
BELLS

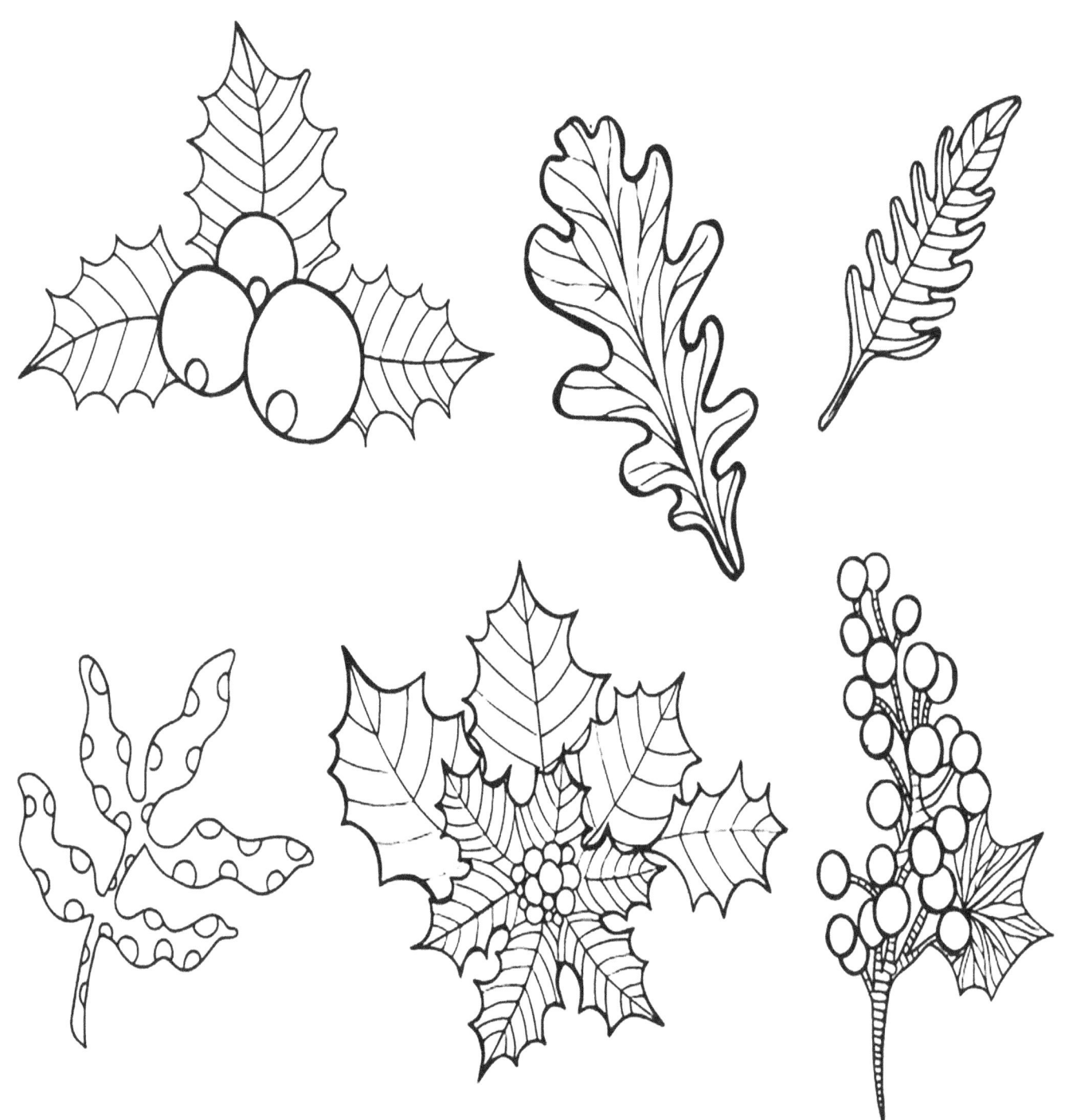

Christmas

Christmas Lamps

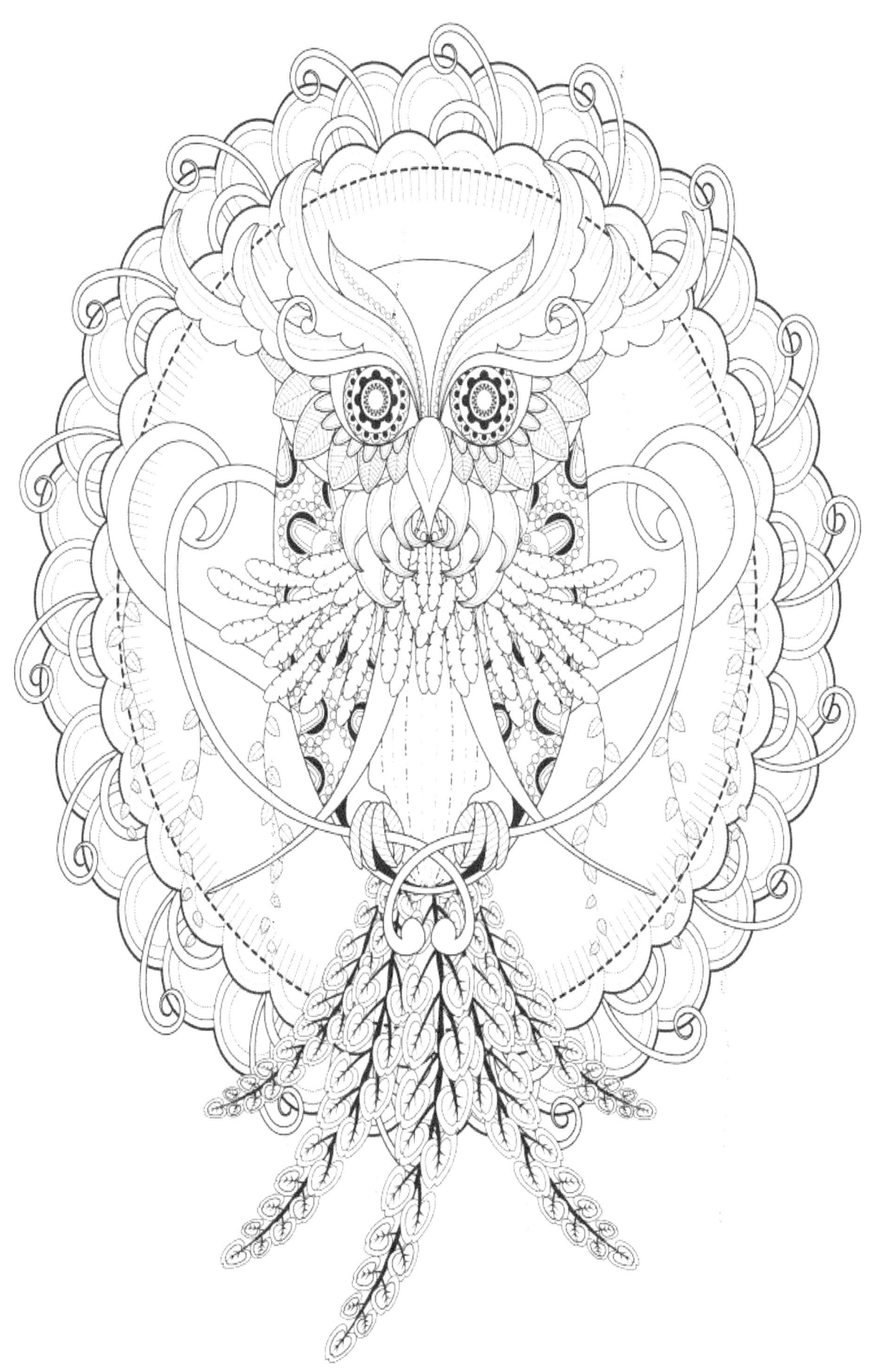

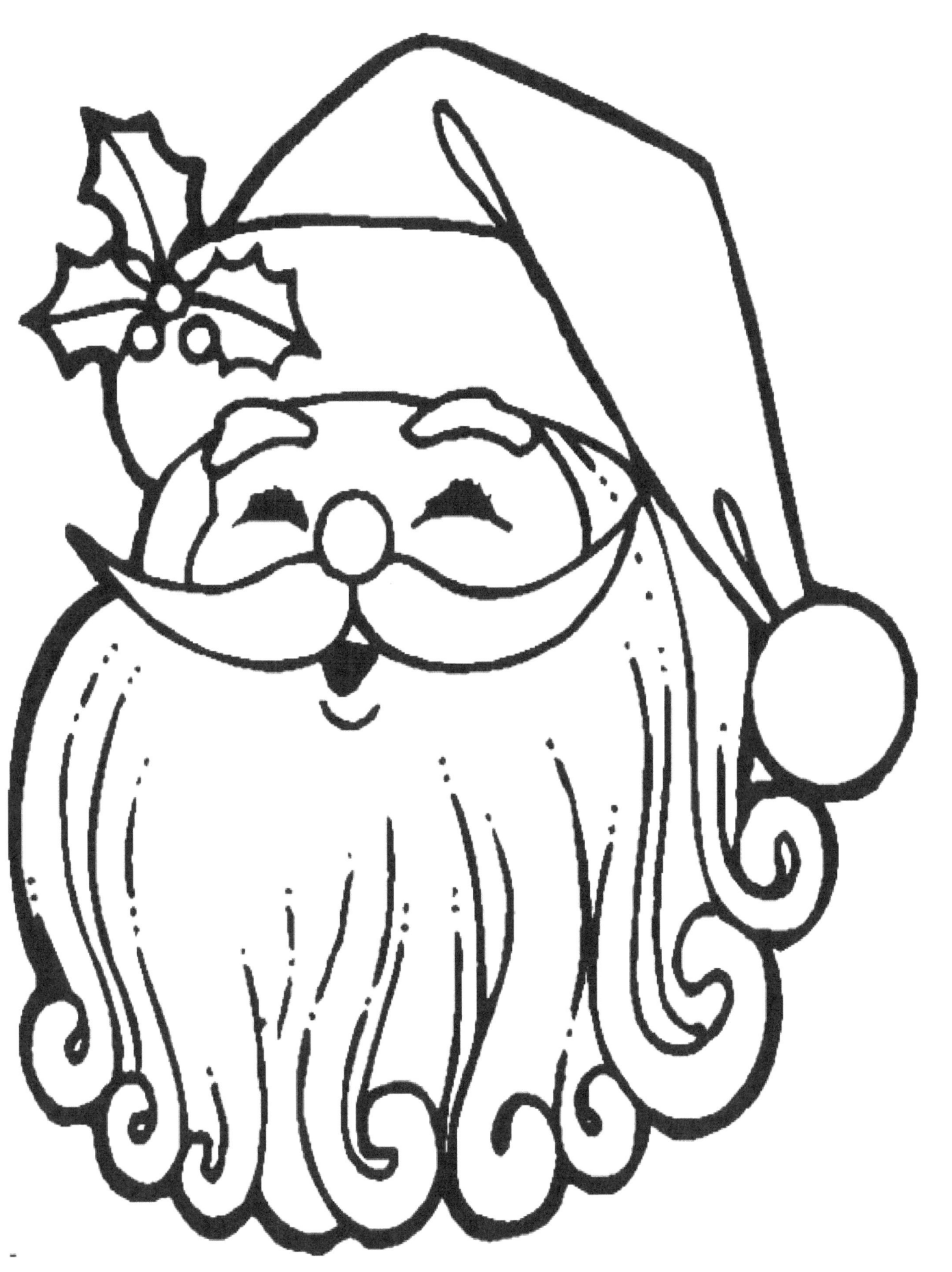

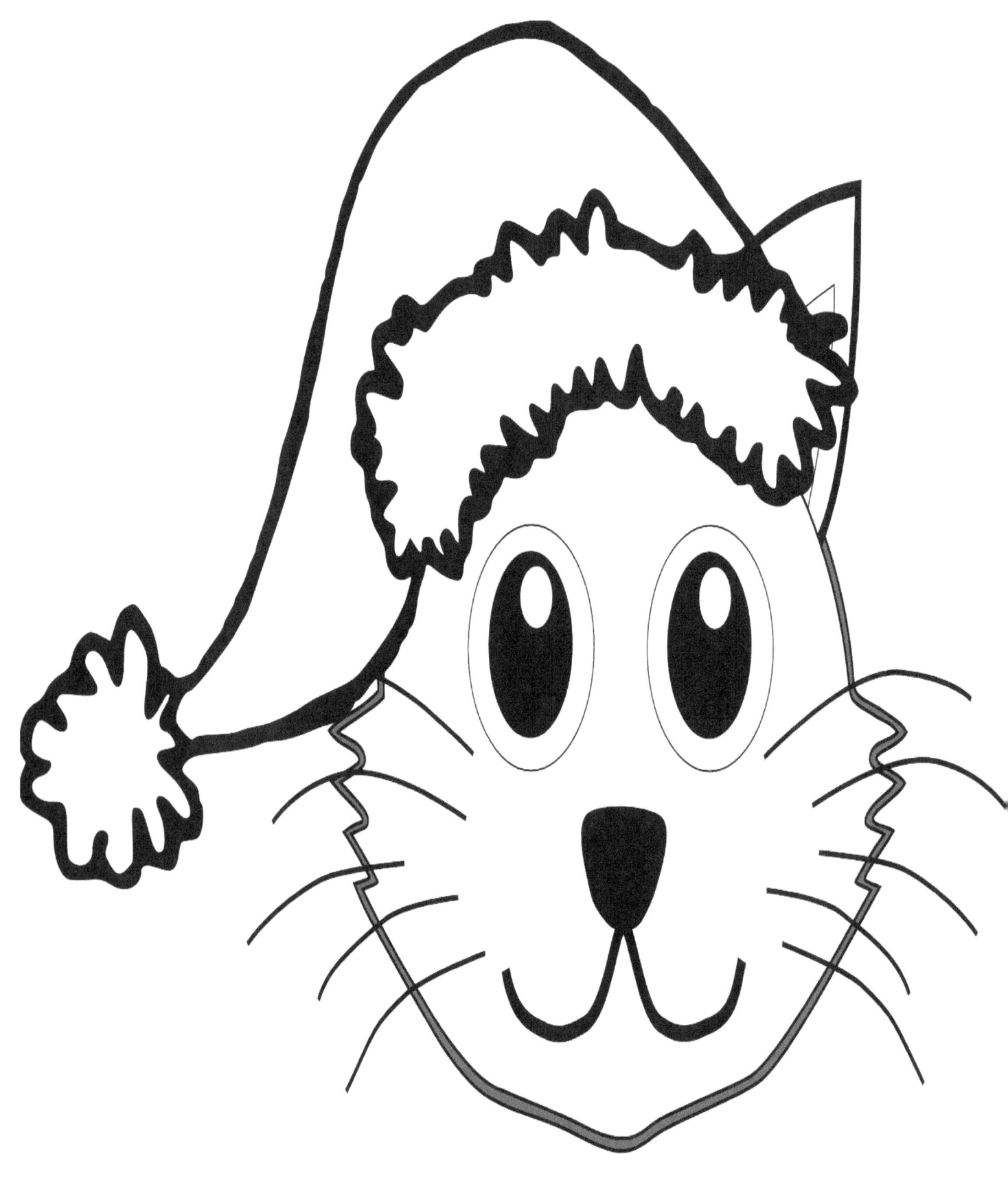

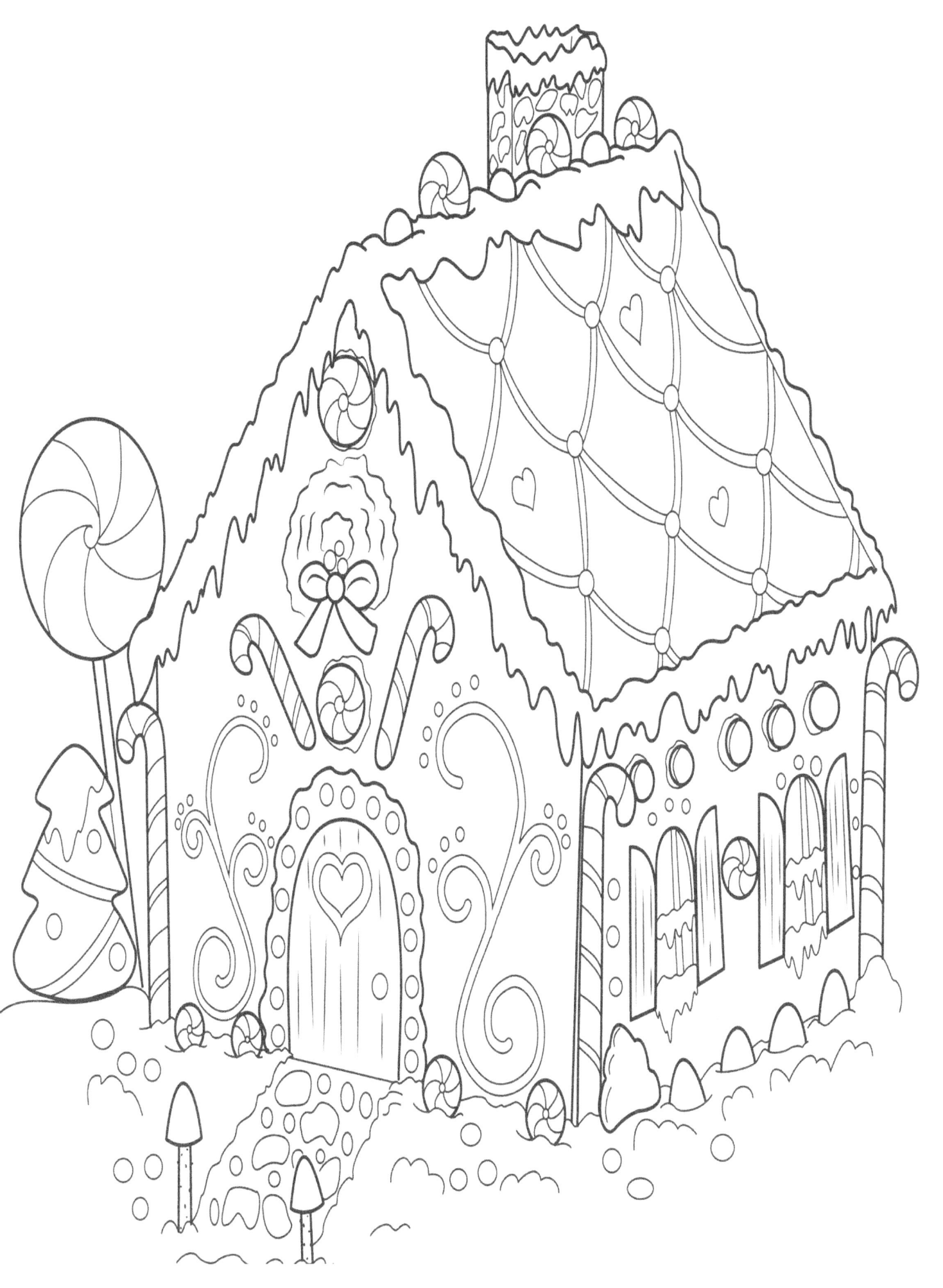

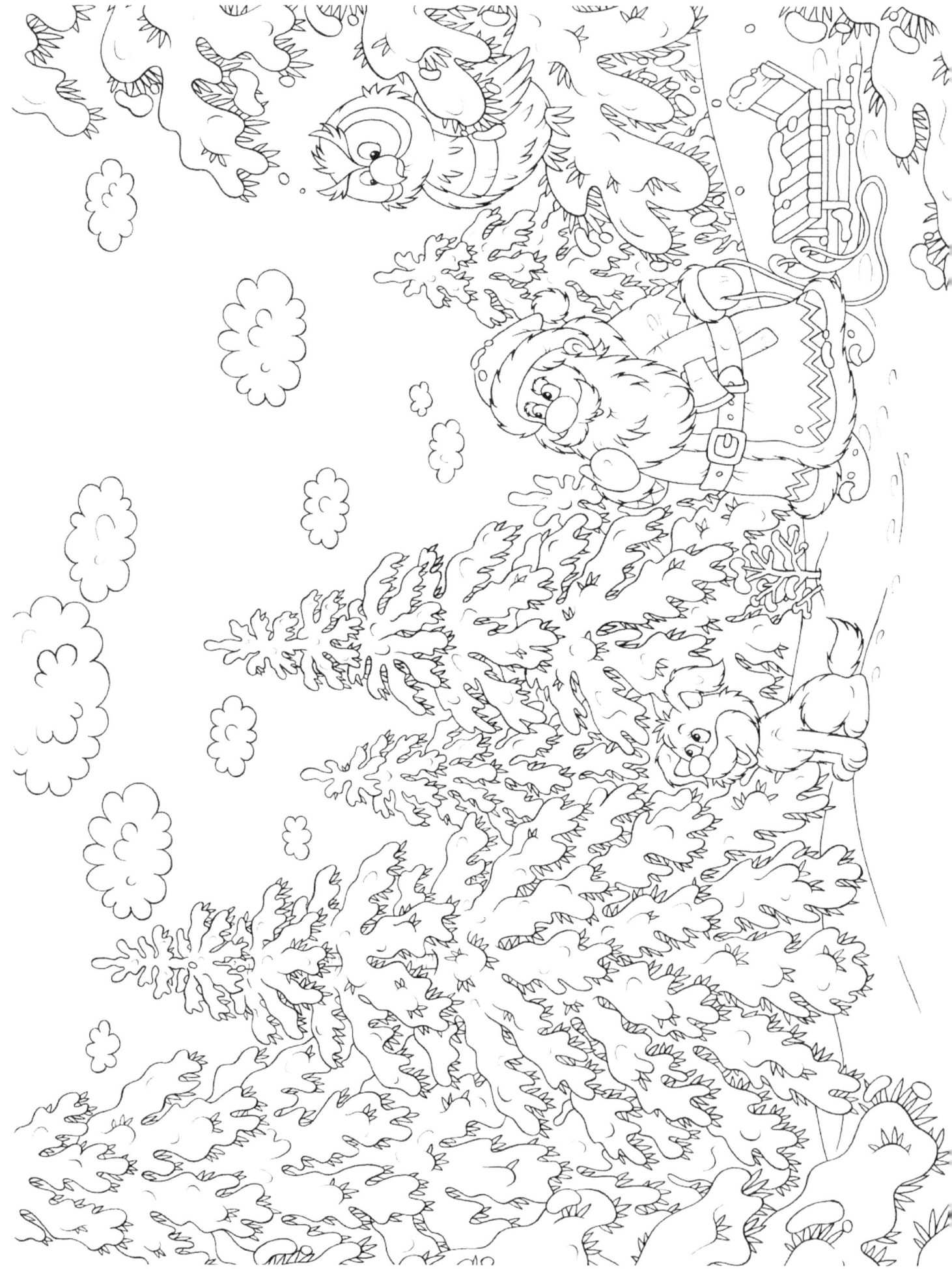

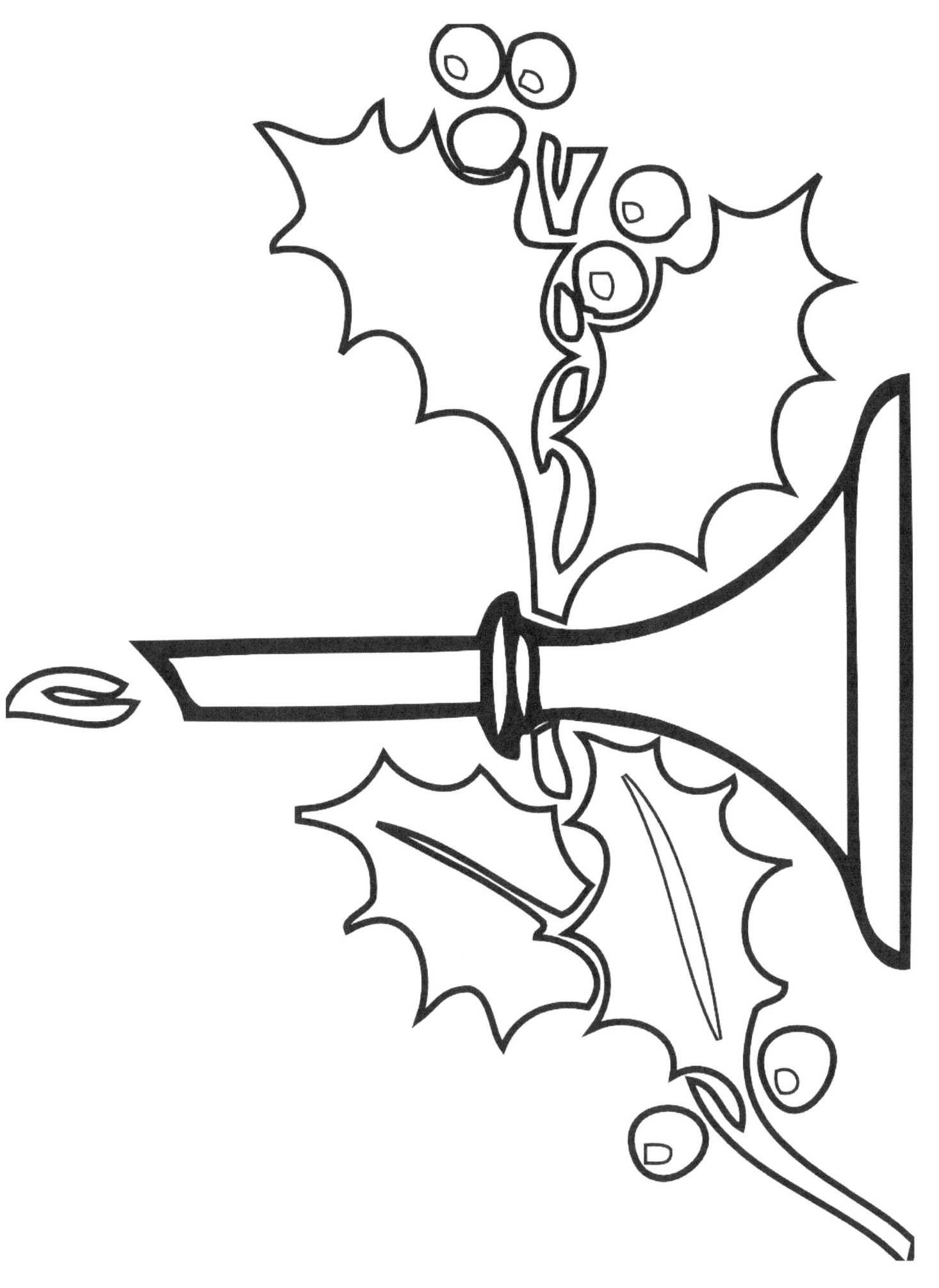

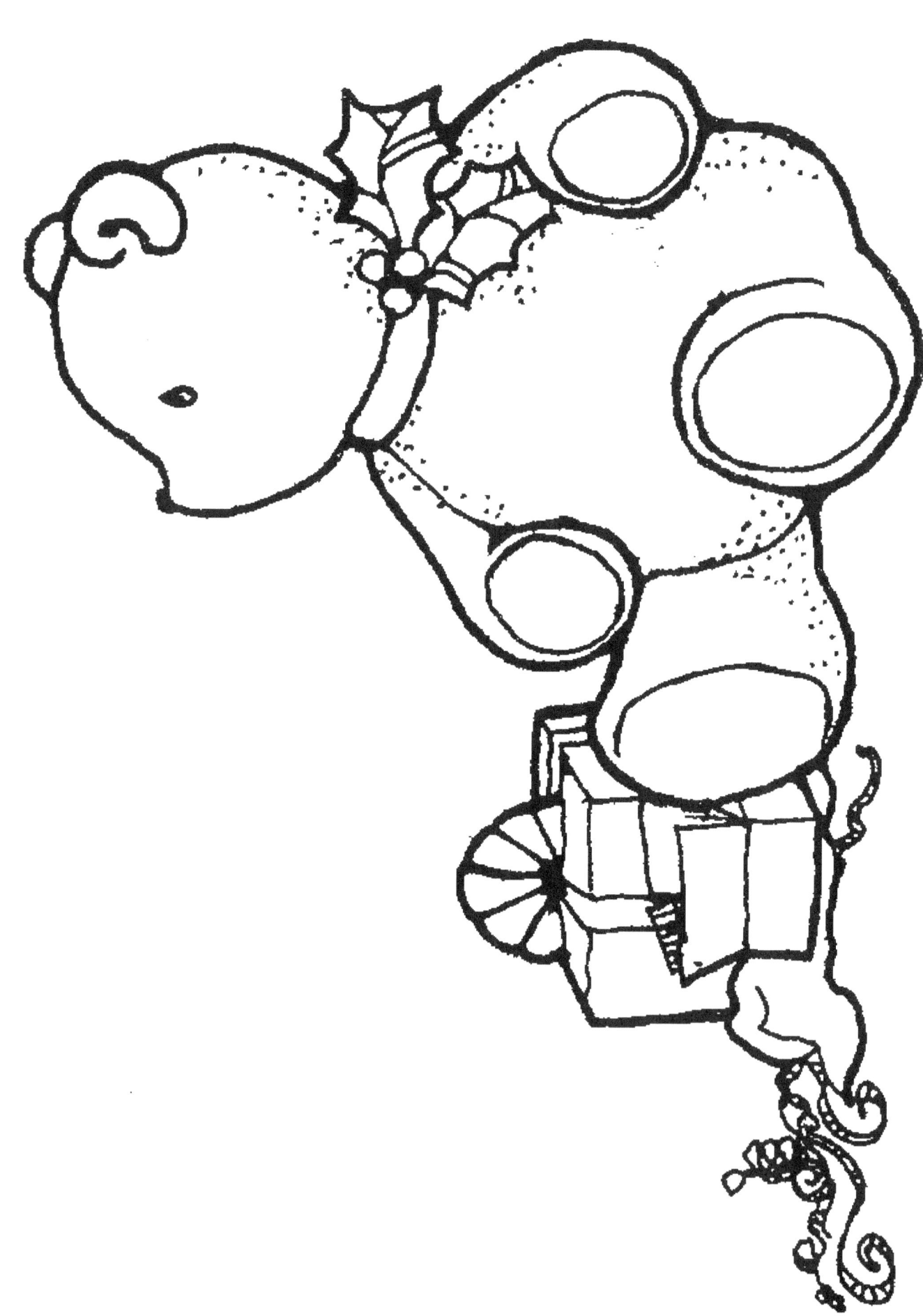

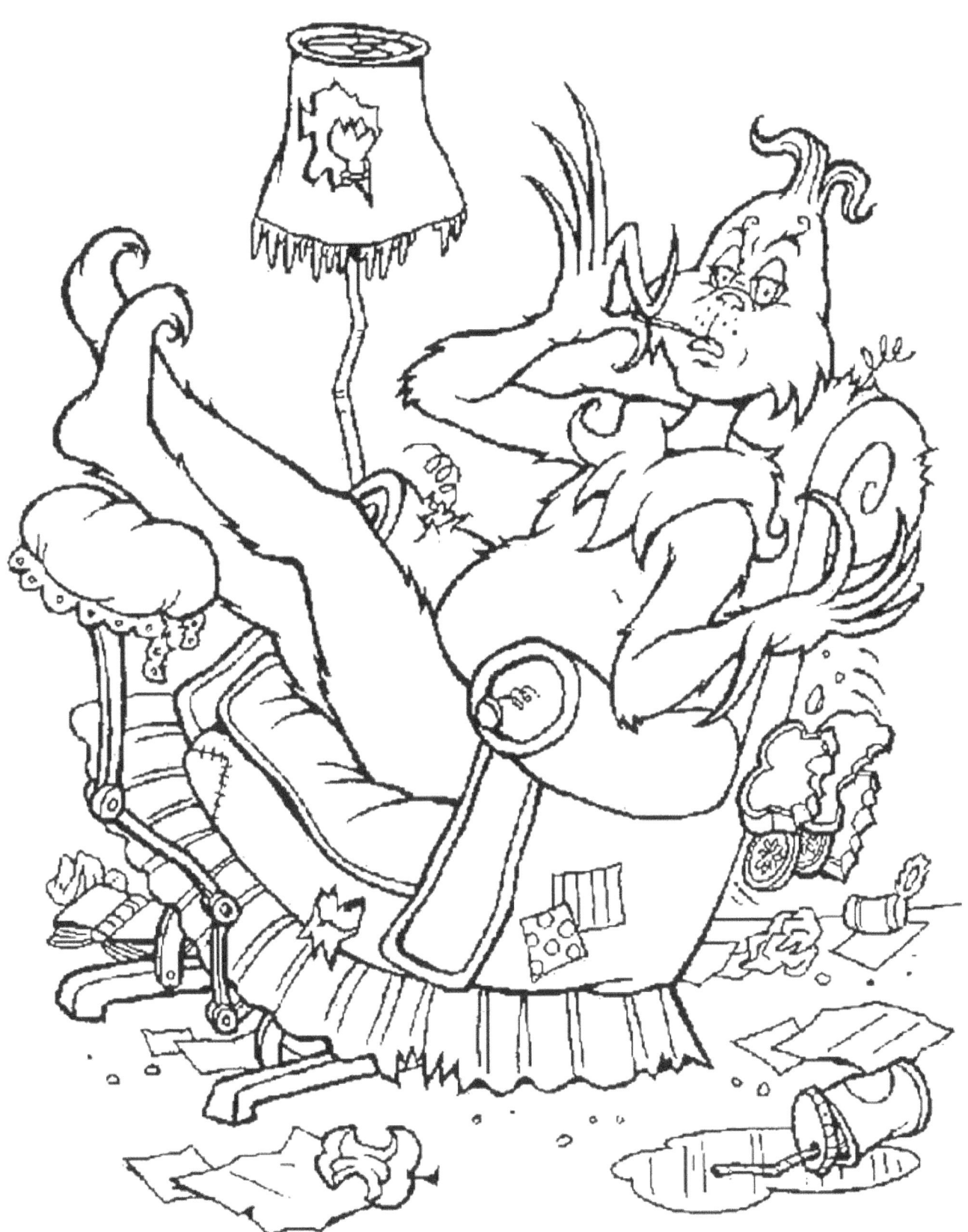

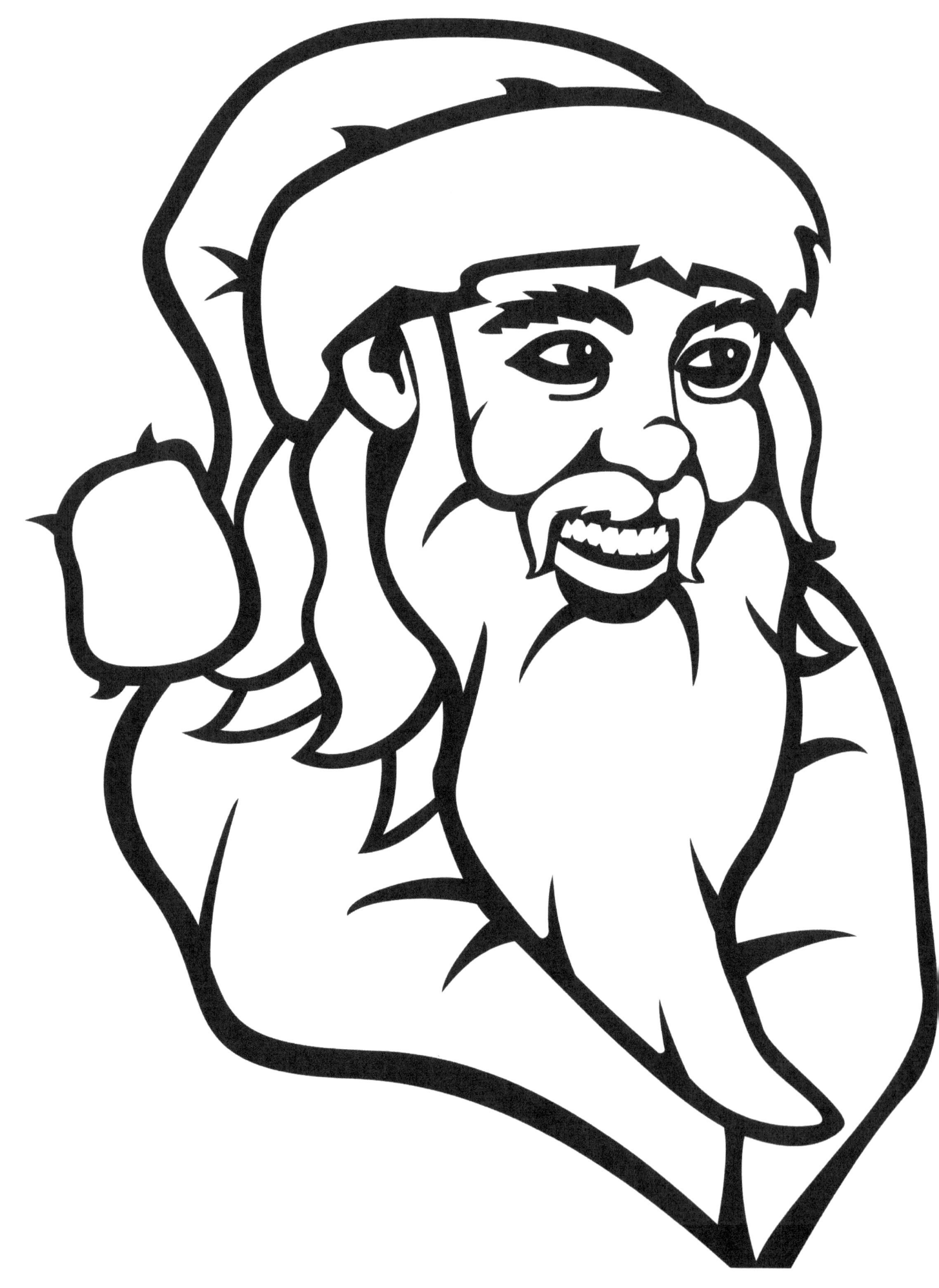

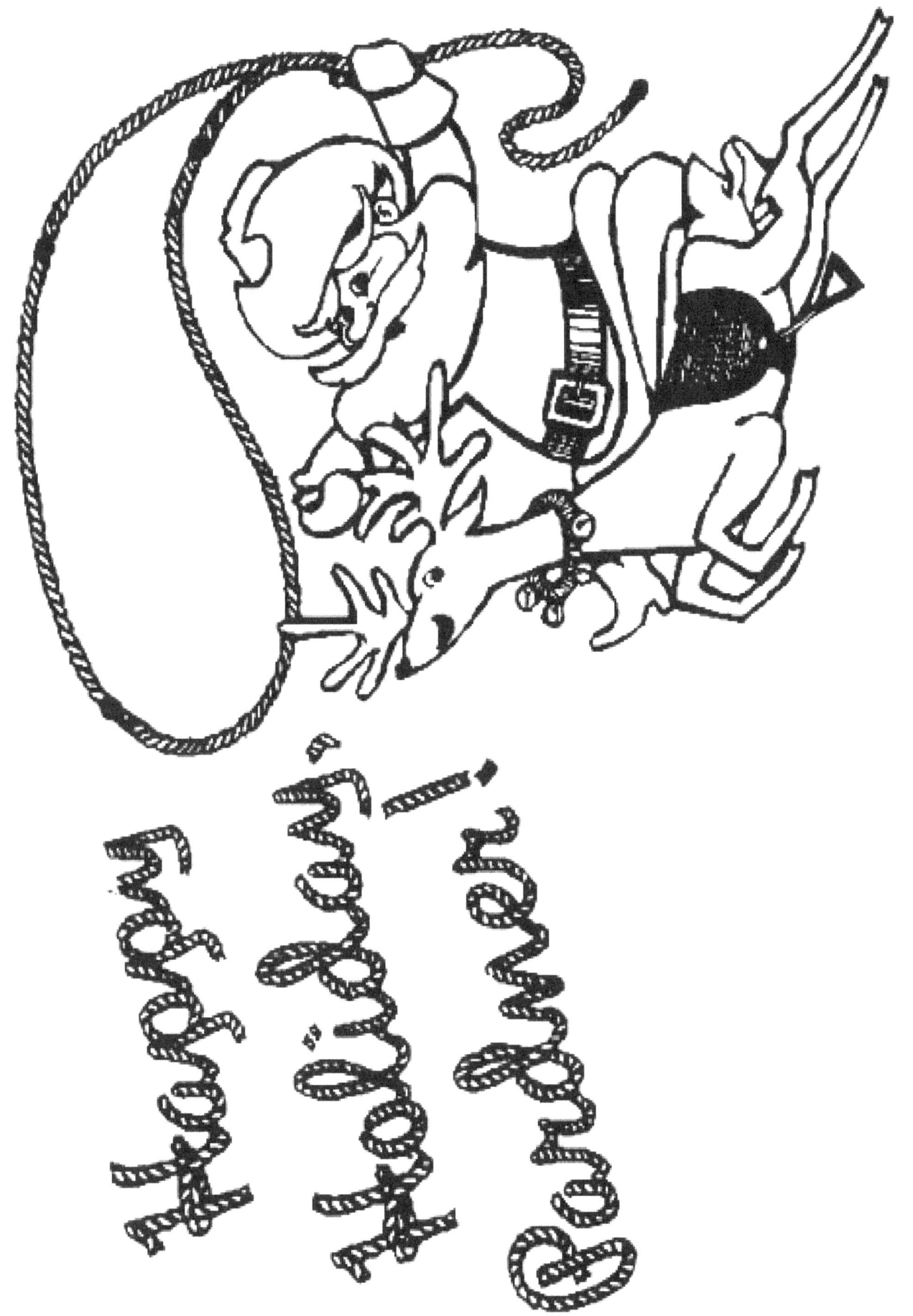

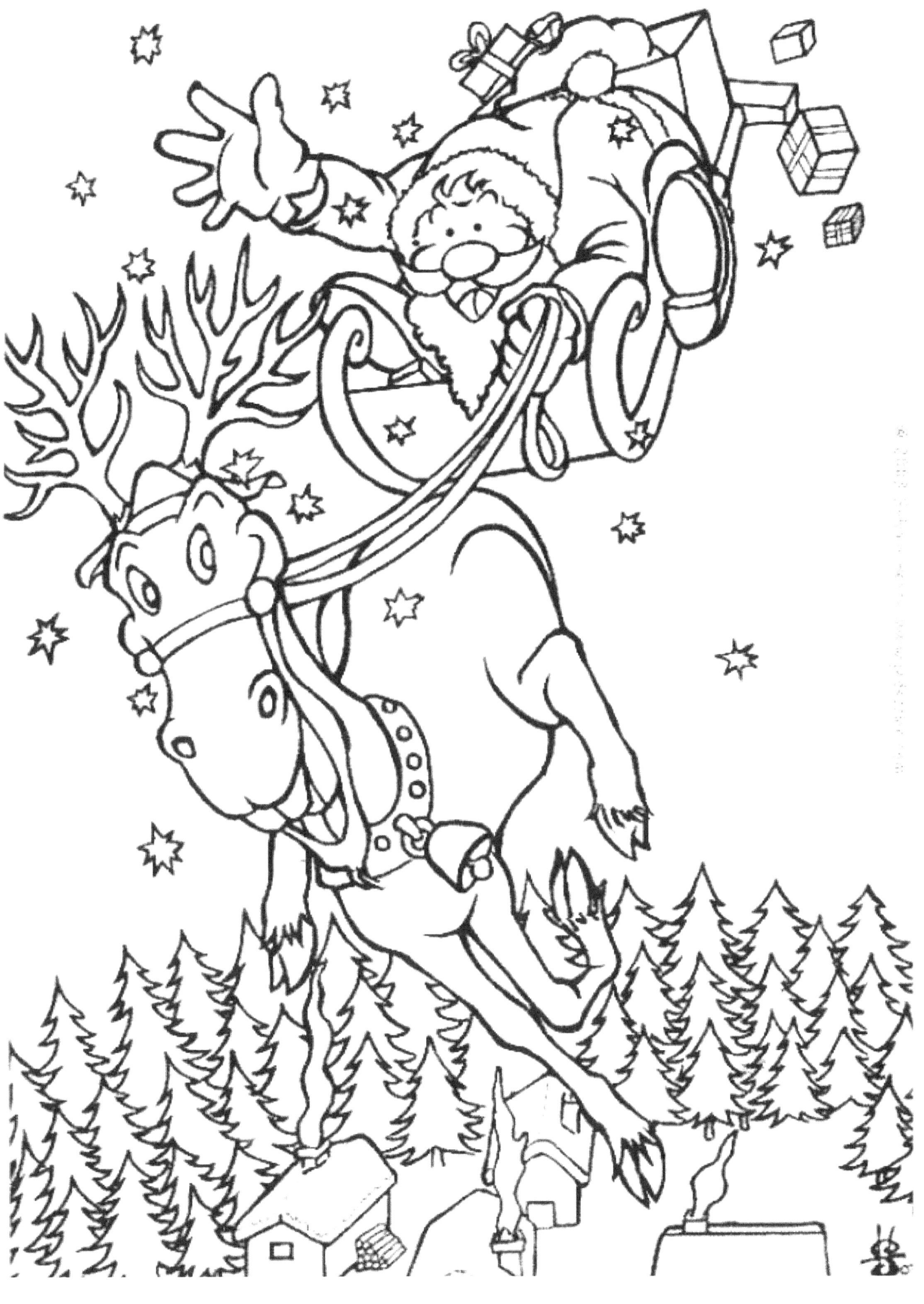

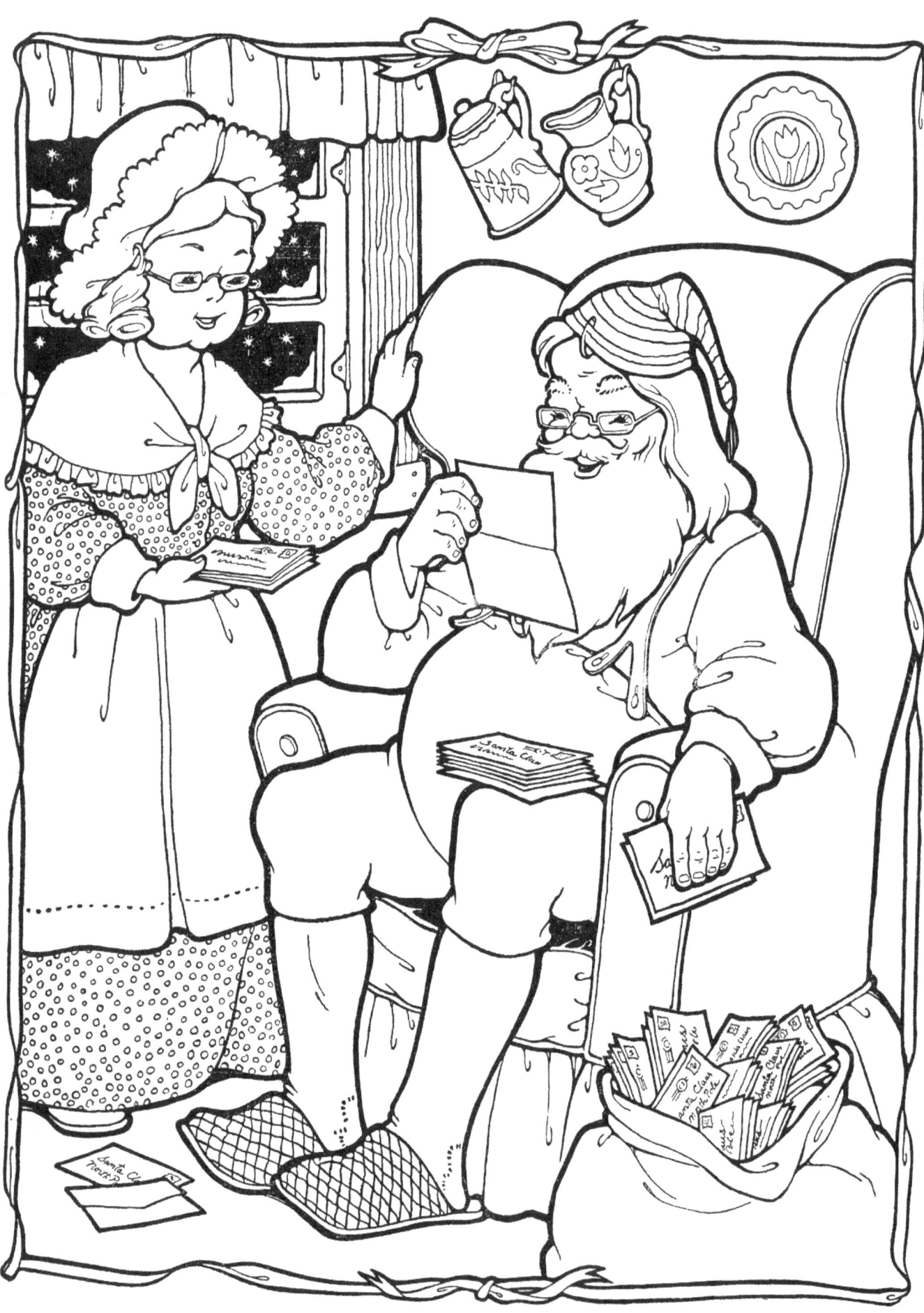

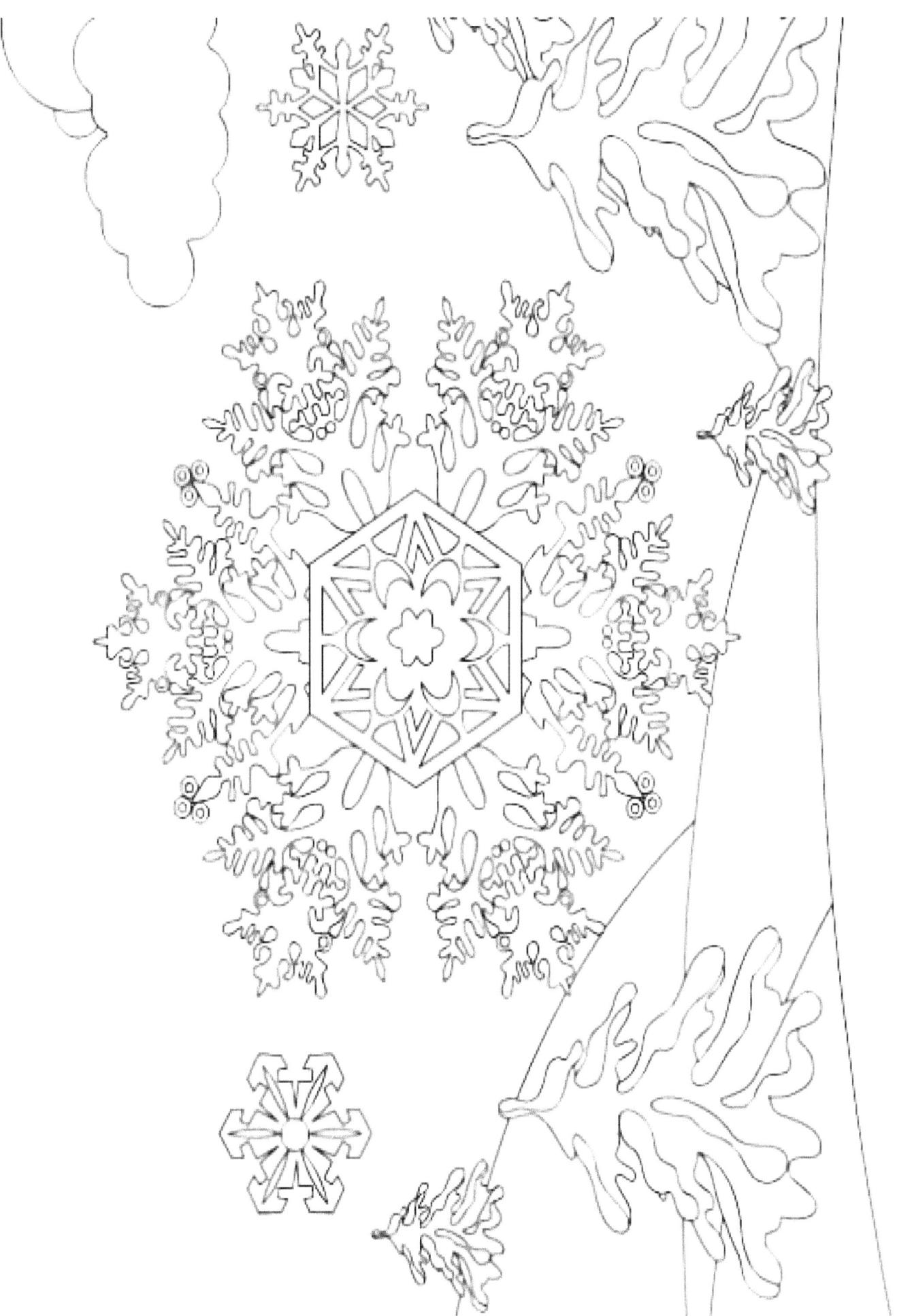

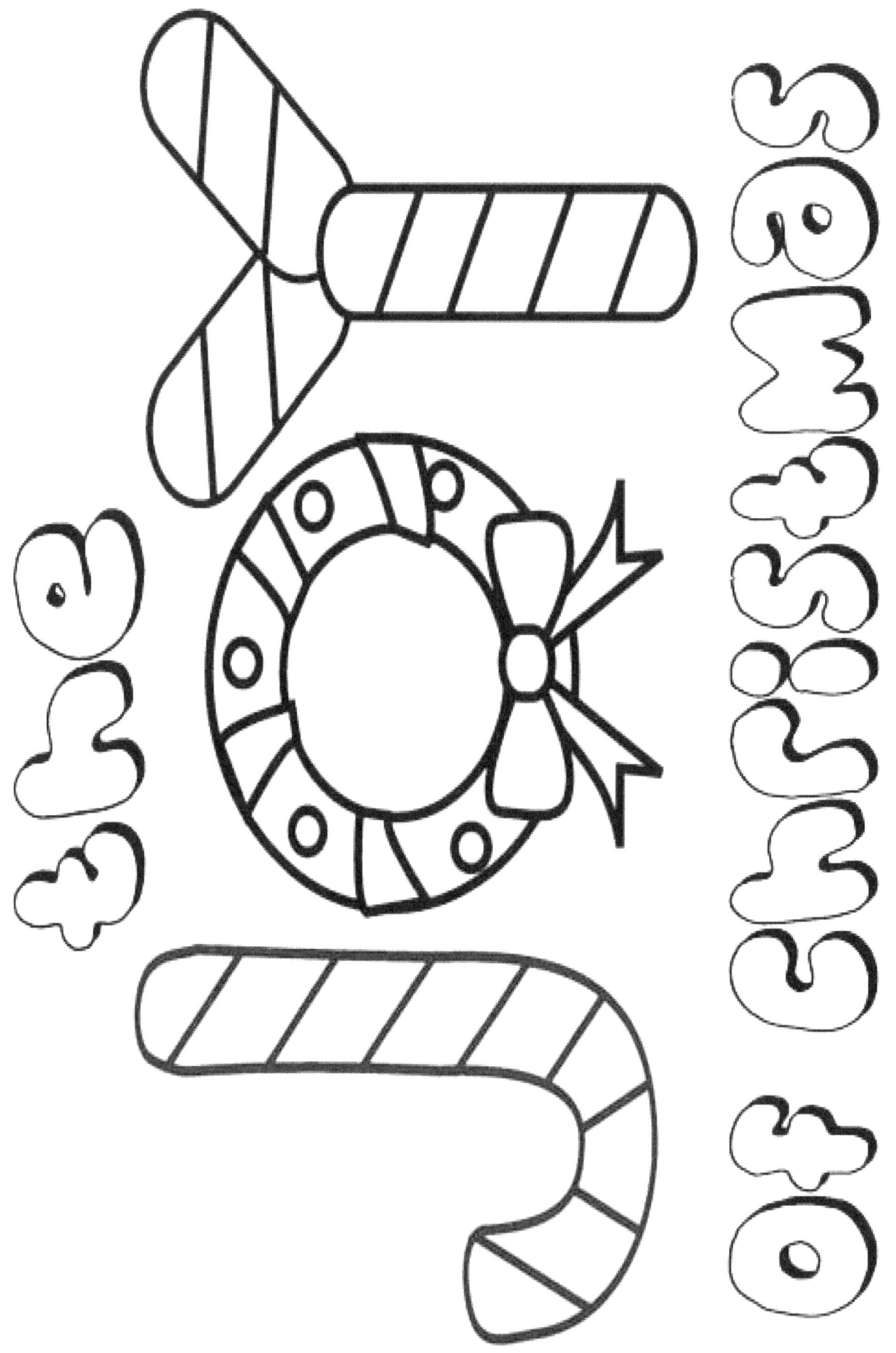

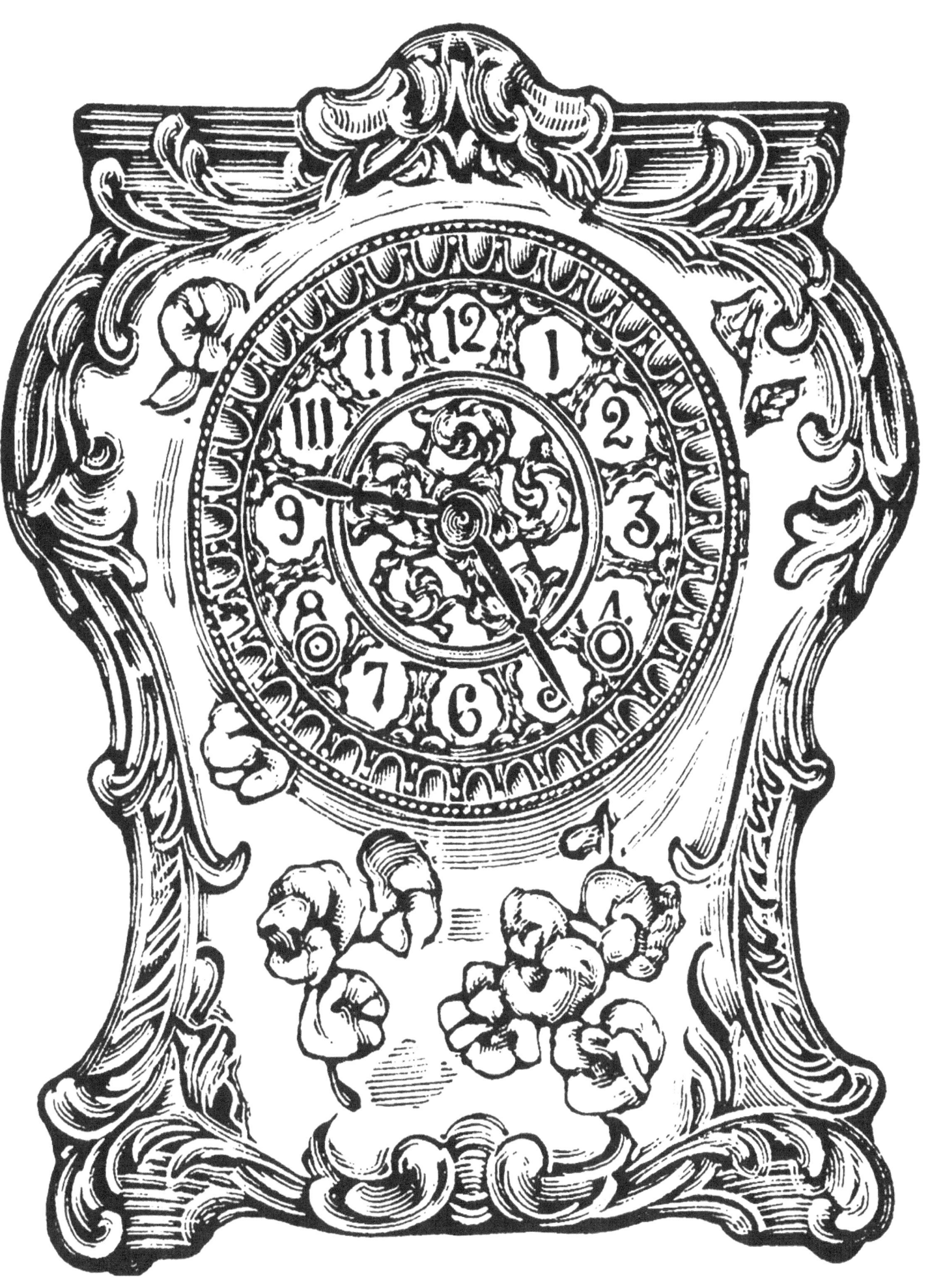

If You Enjoyed This Coloring Book and Would Like More Please Visit The Links Below or Go To RavenswoodPublishing.com

Thank you and Merry Christmas!

ANIMAL MANDALA

https://www.amazon.com/Animal-Mandala-Adult-Coloring-Book/dp/1979322066/ref=sr_1_1?ie=UTF8&qid=1510705463&sr=8-1&keywords=animal+mandala+coloring+book+Kitty+honeycutt

SUGAR SKULLS

https://www.amazon.com/dp/1977994717/ref=sr_1_1?ie=UTF8&qid=1507275242&sr=8-1&keywords=sugar+skulls+coloring+book+Various+Artists

FOR THE LOVE OF CATS

https://www.amazon.com/Love-Cats-Adult-Coloring-Book/dp/198110299X/ref=sr_1_26?ie=UTF8&qid=1511841577&sr=8-26&keywords=FOR+THE+LOVE+OF+CATS+COLORING+BOOK

ALSO CHECK OUT RAVENSWOOD PUBLISHING FOR MORE BOOKS IN ALL GENRES!

http://www.ravenswoodpublishing.com

www.ingramcontent.com/pod-product-compliance
Lightning Source LLC
Chambersburg PA
CBHW080743240526
45472CB00025B/2217